EASY HOME
IMPROVEMENTS

your living room

EASY HOME IMPROVEMENTS

your living room

STEWART WALTON

LEBHAR-FRIEDMAN BOOKS

New York • Chicago • Los Angeles • London • Paris • Tokyo

Lebhar-Friedman Books
425 Park Avenue
New York, NY 10022

First U.S. edition published 2001 by Lebhar-Friedman Books

Published by Lebhar-Friedman Books
Lebhar-Friedman Books is a company of Lebhar-Friedman, Inc.

Printed and bound in China by Excel Printing.
Originated in Singapore by Pica.

Library of Congress Cataloging-in-Publication Data
on file at the Library of Congress.

ISBN: 0-86730-838-9

Project Editor Guy Croton
Designer Glen Wilkins
Editorial Coordinator Caroline Watson
Photographer Alistair Hughes
Managing Editor Antonia Cunningham
Managing Art Editor Phil Gilderdale
Editorial Director Ellen Dupont
Art Director Dave Goodman
Production Amanda Mackie
Indexer Adam Richard§

Front cover photography: **Rodney Weidland/Belle/Arcaid**
Back cover photography: **Alistair Hughes**

Visit our Web site at lfbooks.com

Note

Every effort has been taken to ensure that all information in this book is correct and compatible with national standards generally accepted at the time of publication. For the photographs in this book, both power and hand tools have been positioned as a guide only. Always follow the manufacturer's instructions for any tools, and wear protective clothing and apparatus where recommended. The author and publisher disclaim any liability, loss, injury or damage incurred as a consequence, directly or indirectly, of the use and application of the contents of this book. None of the material in this book may be reproduced without the permission of Marshall Developments Ltd.

contents

introduction

The living room is the heart of every home—the place where people gather and spend the most time, other than in their beds. Nowadays the living room is generally designed and furnished with comfort and relaxation in mind. More often than not it is a warm, comfortable refuge from both the outside world and the more functional, work-orientated rooms of the house, such as the kitchen or home office.

For these reasons, most people spend more time and money decorating and furnishing their living room than any other space in their home. And a very expensive process it can be, which often takes months or even years to complete. Items such as suites, shelving units, tables, and chairs are generally big and expensive to acquire. Sometimes, furnishing a living room can be more about fulfilling essential priorities as quickly as possible, rather than choosing the furnishings you really want, simply because of lack of funds.

One solution to this commonplace problem is to decorate your living room yourself and construct your own furniture. It is not as difficult as you might think and a lot, lot cheaper... This book is packed full of ideas and stylish projects for a better, more attractive living room, whatever the size or style of your home. It will save you money and give you the added satisfaction of letting you surround yourself with things you made yourself in your main living space. By choosing your own colors and fabrics, you can also personalize your space.

The projects in this book range from basic decorating techniques such as hanging wallpaper and putting up a dado rail to the construction of ambitious individual items of furniture, such as a collector's display case or an open shelf unit. Other projects show you how to make the most of a recess or awkward corner in your living room—such as the alcove shelving on pages 18–27—or how to enhance existing furniture and decor with stylish soft furnishings such as cushion covers or tab-topped curtains.

All the projects included in this book were designed to be accessible to as wide a range of people as possible, so none of them are especially difficult to make. Each project is graded with a rough skill rating of "Beginner," "Intermediate," or "Advanced," to help you select the items most suited to your own abilities, backed-up with a rough indication of how long the project should take to make and full details of all the materials and tools required. No specialist skills are needed—the main considerations to keep in mind when making most of these projects are being patient and taking your time. With careful attention to any manufacturer's instructions and standard safety precautions, and the use of good quality tools and protective clothing, you should not encounter any real difficulties in constructing something special and a little different for your living room.

I hope you get as much satisfaction out of making these projects and practicing the various techniques as I did in preparing them for this book. Enjoy these projects.

Stewart Walton

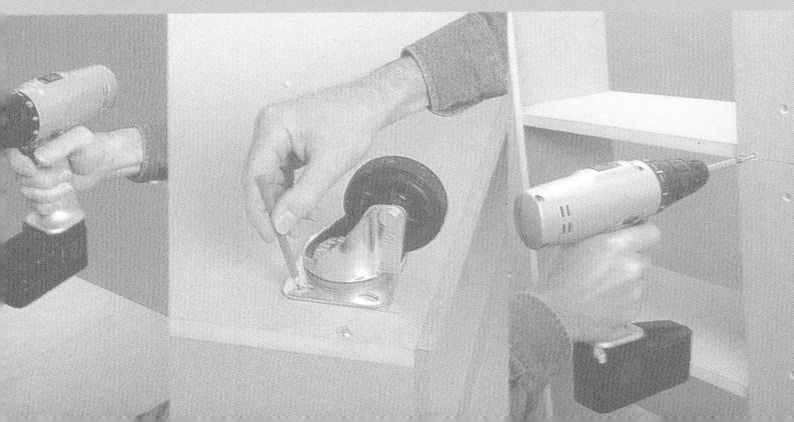

chapter 1 *Storage*

1. Making an open-shelving unit

2. Fitting alcove shelving

3. Building a display case

making an open-shelving unit

This project offers an elegant and slightly unusual alternative to the many standard open-shelving units now available. It is also considerably less expensive than they are to buy, and provides the additional fulfilment of knowing that you have constructed a centerpiece item of furniture for the most important family room in your home. Take extra special care with your joints when making this one, and be sure that everything in your construction squares up properly.

Materials (all lumber is softwood unless otherwise stated)

Back uprights: 2 pieces of MDF ½ x 5½ x 64¼ in.

Base dividers: 2 pieces of MDF ¾ x 9 x 15 in.

Middle dividers: 6 pieces of MDF ¾ x 9 x 12 in.

Top dividers: 2 pieces of MDF ¾ x 9 x 10½ in.

Shelves: 4 pieces of MDF ¾ x 9 x 31 in.

No. 6 (1½ in.) screws • Wood filler • Paint or varnish

Tools

Workbench • Tape measure • Rule • Combination square • Carpenter's pencil • Power drill with screw, countersinking, ⅙ in., and ⅛ in. bits • Filling knife • Fine-grade abrasive paper and sanding block • Paint brush

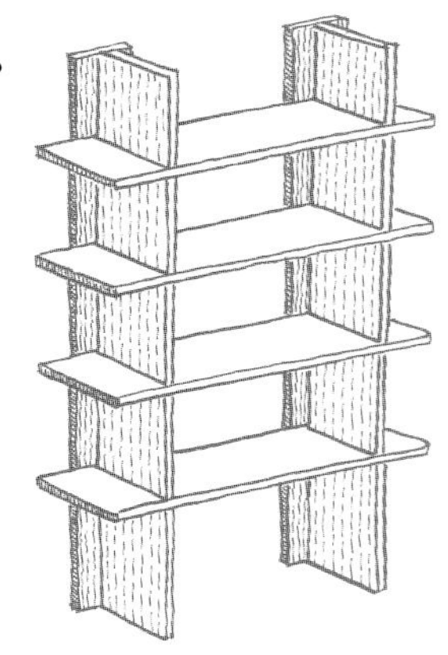

Skill level

Intermediate

Time

8 hours

1 Measure and cut all the pieces to the dimensions given in the list of materials. Lay the two back uprights flat on the work surface. Carefully measure and mark a line down the center of each of the uprights, 3 in. in from each edge. Next, measure the width of the MDF board used in this project—¾ in.—across the center lines you have just drawn, and draw two equidistant additional lines ⅜ in. to each side of the center lines to mark where the divider pieces will be attached to the center of the uprights.

2 Butt the two uprights together side by side and check that their bottom ends are flush. Use the matched pairs of upright shelf dividers to measure and mark off the horizontal fixing positions of the four shelves on the back uprights, allowing for the ¾-in. thickness of each shelf between the dividers. Ensure that the dividers are in their pairs before making your marks.

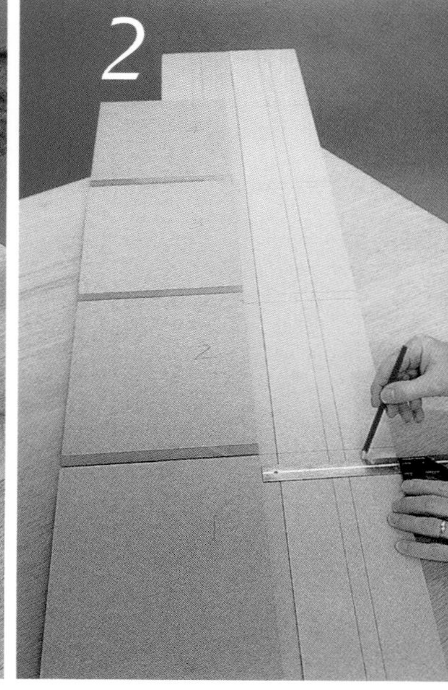

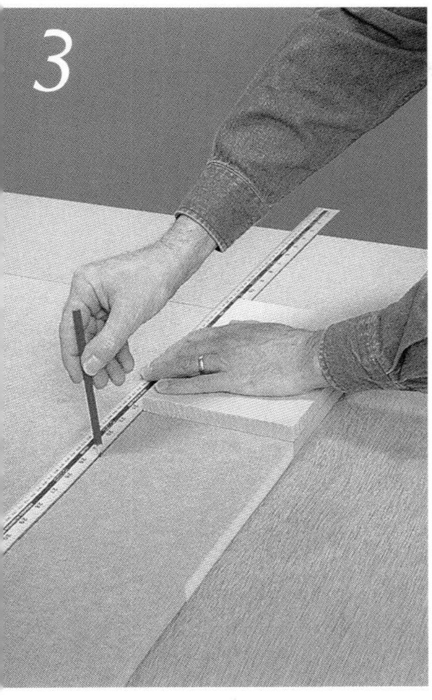

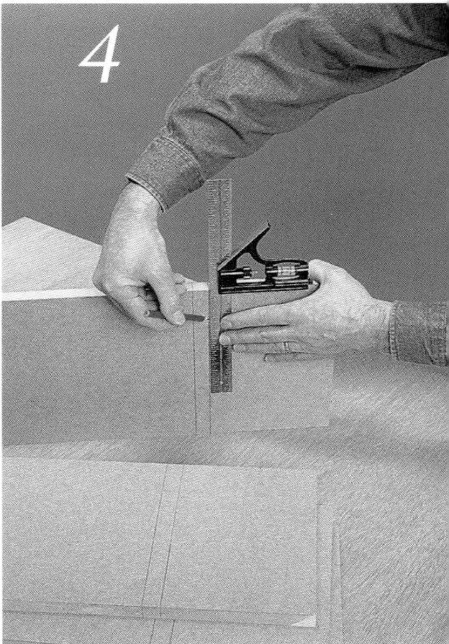

3 Lay the four shelves down on the workbench and butt them together, side by side, with their ends flush. Use a cut-off piece of ¾ in. MDF, a rule, and a pencil to mark the centerpoints of the two uprights on the tops of the shelves. These should be positioned so that 5 in. of shelf will protrude from the outside edge of each upright once the unit has been assembled.

4 Use a combination square and pencil to transfer the fixing guidelines from the tops of the four shelves over their back edges and onto their bottom surfaces. Ensure that the marks are in exactly the same positions on both sides. Mark as accurately as you can at all stages to ensure a good fit on assembly.

5 Mark two evenly spaced fixing points at each end of every shelf in the center of the fixing guidelines. These mark where the divider pieces will be attached to the shelves. Each fixing point should be positioned 2 in. in from the front or back edge of the shelf. Drill ⅙ in. clearance holes through the entire thickness of the shelves.

6 To strengthen the unit, each divider piece will be attached to all adjoining shelves and divider pieces. This means that most of the dividers will have a screw driven into them from below at one end and from above at the other. For this reason, countersink only one hole at each end of every shelf from its top side. The other hole will be countersunk from the underside of the shelf.

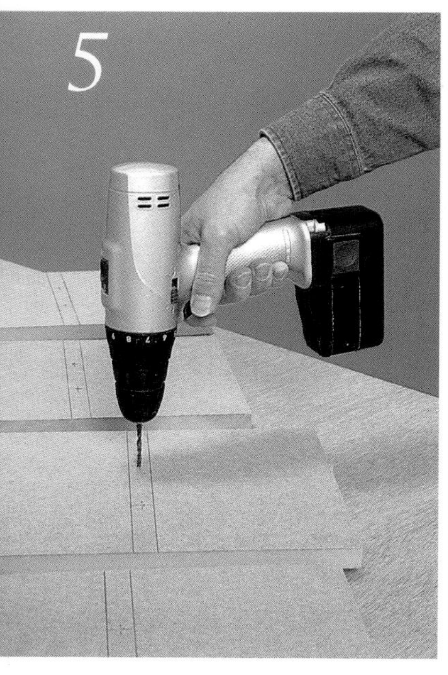
5

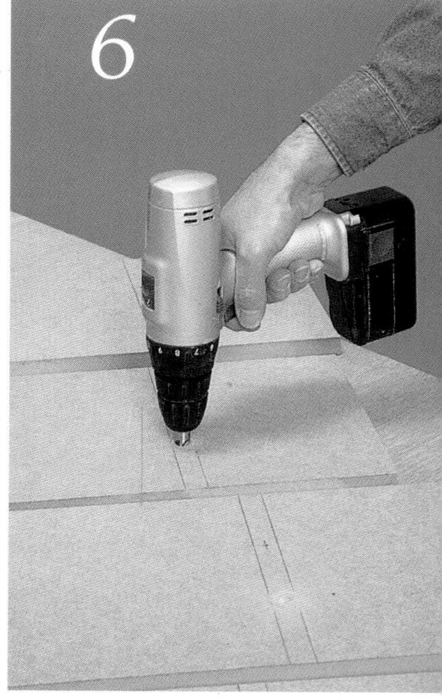
6

7 Turn all four shelves over on the workbench and countersink the other hole, at the back of each shelf, from the underside of the shelves. You should now have four shelves with two evenly spaced holes at each end, one hole countersunk from each side.

8 The next step is to begin fixing the four shelves to the ten divider pieces. Keep the dividers in their matched pairs. Start with the pair of base dividers, holding them up in line with the fixing holes on the first shelf. Clamp a spare piece of MDF to the shelf to assist you in holding the divider piece in the right position against the shelf. Drill two $\frac{1}{8}$ in. pilot holes into the top and bottom edges of the divider piece through the clearance holes that you drilled into the shelves in step 5. Repeat this process with all the shelves and dividers.

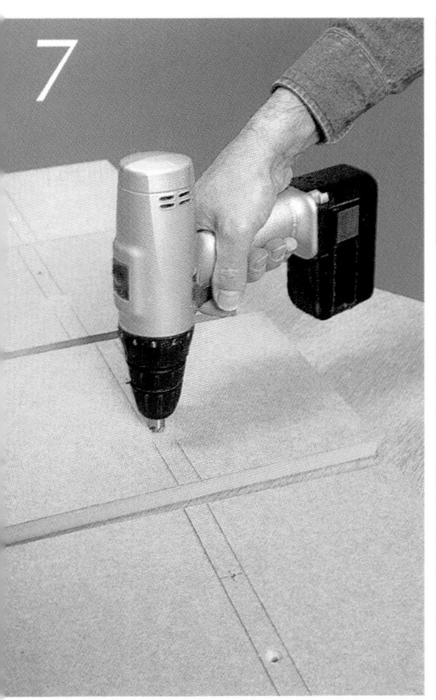

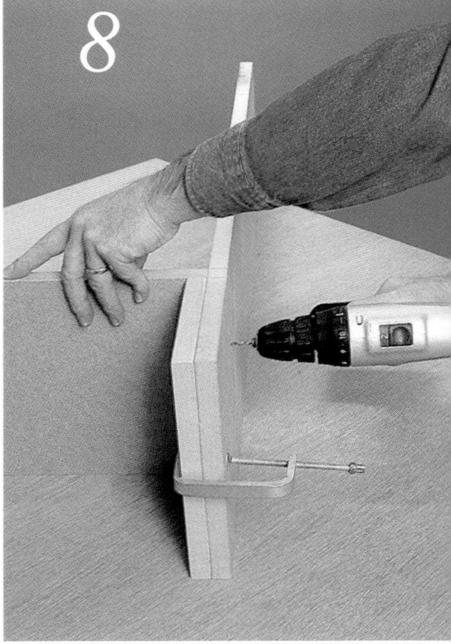

9 Use No. 6 (1½ in.) screws to begin attaching the dividers to the shelves. At first, drive only one screw into the end of each divider through the countersunk hole in the underside of the shelf that will be positioned below it. As you do this, keep the off-cut piece of MDF clamped to the shelf to ensure that the divider will be held square-on to the shelf as you drive in the first screws (as shown).

10 Once all the dividers have been attached to all the shelves with one screw each from their undersides, begin attaching the dividers to the shelves from their top sides. Using the clamped piece of offcut MDF as a guide once more, swivel each of the dividers in turn on their one fixing screw and drive a second screw into the divider below from the top side of the shelf above, as shown. Repeat the process until all the dividers and top shelf uprights have been secured to the shelves with two screws each.

11 The next step is to attach the two back uprights to the assembled shelves and dividers. Stand the assembled shelves and dividers upright on the floor. Place the uprights in position behind them, so that the fixing guidelines on the centers of the uprights marked in step 1 align perfectly with the fixing guidelines marked on the backs of the shelves in step 3. Drill a 1/6 in. clearance hole through each upright 2 in. above and 2 in. below each shelf. Stop before you drill into the dividers.

12 Drill 1/8 in. pilot holes into the backs of the dividers through the clearance holes that you drilled in the uprights in step 11. Drill two further, evenly spaced, horizontal holes through the back uprights and into the backs of the shelves. Use No. 6 (1½ in.) screws to attach the uprights to the shelves and dividers. Fill, sand, and paint or varnish as necessary, and your open shelf unit is ready for use.

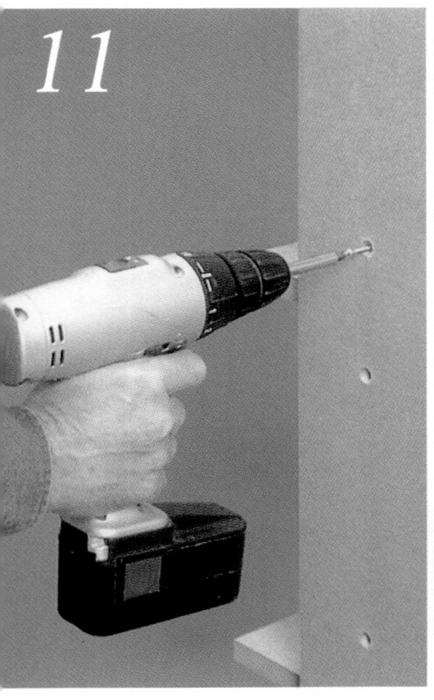

11

12

fitting alcove shelving

Many living rooms have an awkward corner or little recess that presents a problem when you are furnishing your home. Often the best solution is to transform it into a feature of your living room by installing attractive alcove shelving. This project shows you how to maximize space and create an attractive decorative feature.

Materials

Shelf: 1 piece of MDF 1 in. x width and depth of alcove
Back wall batten: 1 piece of PAR 1 x 1 x in. x width of alcove
Side wall battens: 2 pieces of PAR 1 x 1 in. x depth of alcove
Shelf edging: 1 length of PAR ½ x 2 x in. x width of shelf
No. 6 (3 in.) screws • No. 6 (1½ in.) screws • 1 in. panel pins • Wall plugs • Wood glue • Wood filler • Can of paint or varnish

Tools

Workbench • Hand saw • Miter saw • Power drill with ¼ in., ⅙ in., screw, and countersinking bits • Spirit level • Rule • Tape measure • Combination square • Adjustable protractor • Hand screwdriver • Hammer • Filling knife • Fine-grade abrasive paper and sanding block • Paint brushes

Skill level

Intermediate

Time

4 hours

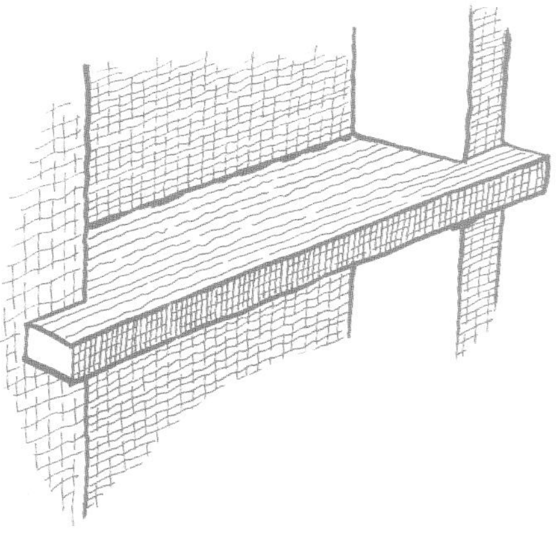

1 Select the alcove or recess where you wish to put your shelf and decide on the height it should be from the floor. Use a measure and spirit level to ascertain the position of the support batten for the shelf on the back wall of the alcove. Draw a line along the spirit level to mark the position of the top of the shelf support batten.

2 Use the spirit level, measure, and pencil to transfer the shelf support fixing guideline to the two side walls of the alcove. Again, check that the lines are perfectly straight with the spirit level and ensure that they align with the first guideline on the back wall.

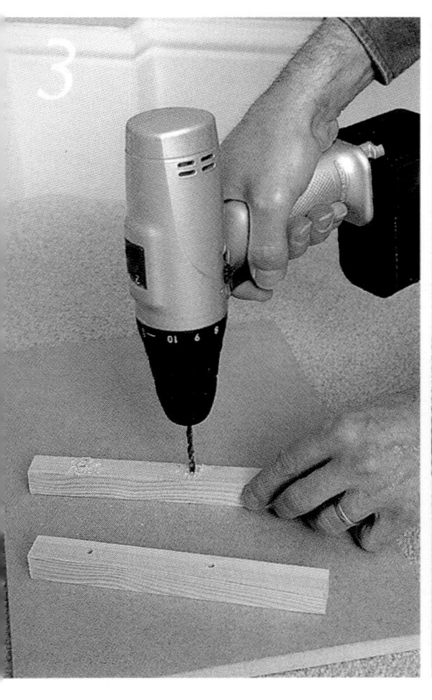

3 Measure and cut the two side wall battens to fit using a hand saw. Allow for any "reveal" in the alcove—that is, any wall extending beyond the alcove—as you mark off the lengths of the side wall battens. (See steps 8 and 9.) Mark two suitably spaced fixing points in the centers of each batten with a pencil. Use a power drill and ⅙ in. bit to drill pilot holes through the thickness of the battens. Place a piece of scrap wood underneath the battens as you drill, to prevent making holes in your work surface.

4 Hold the side battens in position up against the wall. Use a bradawl to mark fixing positions on the wall through the screw holes that you drilled in step 3. Press hard with the bradawl to ensure that it makes distinct marks on the side walls. Repeat steps 3 and 4 with the back wall batten, marking and drilling three evenly spaced fixing holes for this longer piece.

5 Use a power drill and ¼ in. drill bit to drill holes at each point marked on the walls with the bradawl. Drill the holes to the depth of the wall plugs that will receive the screws (1½ in.). Remove any debris from the holes with a small brush.

6 Use a hammer to tap a plastic wall plug into each hole that you drilled in step 5. Be careful not to damage the wall decor as you knock the wall plugs into the holes. Ensure that the heads of the wall plugs are flush with the walls.

5

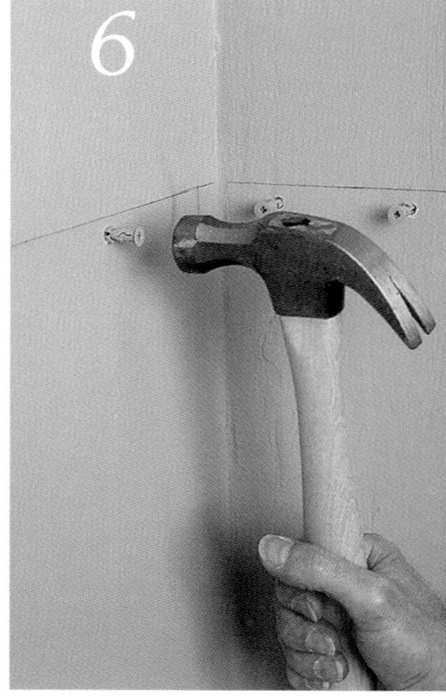
6

7 Use the power drill with a screwdriver bit and No. 6 (3 in.) screws to attach the back and side battens to the walls of the alcove. Ensure that the pilot holes in your battens align perfectly with the plugs in the walls before driving in the screws.

8 Take the alcove shelf and hold it up against the battens on the walls. Use a pencil to mark the lines of cut necessary to make the shelf fit as tightly into the alcove as possible. Use a combination square to draw the lines squarely across the ends of the shelf. If your alcove has a "reveal" at one end—that is, an additional external corner—be sure to allow for this in your calculations as you mark up the shelf. (In the example illustrated, the shelf will fit the alcove and then continue around the corner of the reveal, beyond the edge of the alcove.)

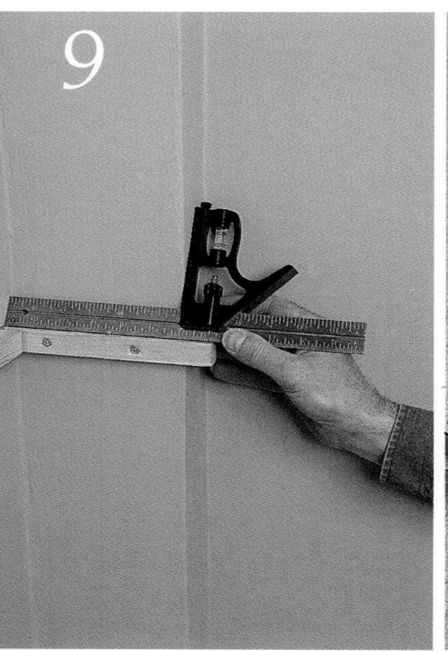

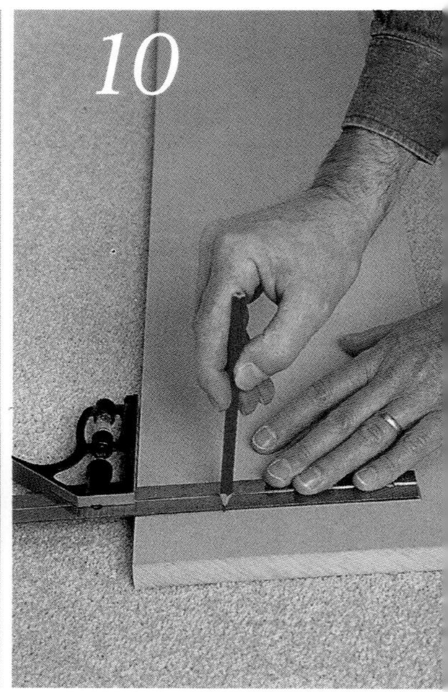

9 If your alcove features a reveal like the one illustrated, use a combination square to measure the depth of the reveal (as shown). Any reveal should have been allowed for in the lengths of the side wall battens cut in step 3. The part of the shelf that extends around the reveal of the alcove will need to be at least partly supported by the protruding side wall battens.

10 Use the combination square and pencil to transfer the reveal depth measurement to the back corner of the shelf (as shown). It is essential to measure and draw the guidelines for the reveal onto the shelf as accurately as possible. If the reveal is not properly allowed for, the shelf will not fit tightly around it at the end of the alcove.

11 If your walls are not perfectly square, there is a good chance that any reveal at the end of your alcove will not be square either, as with the example illustrated here. Use an adjustable protractor and pencil to measure the angle of the reveal as thoroughly as you measured its depth with the combination square in step 10.

12 Again, carefully and accurately transfer your measurements to the back corner of the shelf, where it will meet the reveal. Measure and draw your pencil guidelines until you are completely satisfied that the shelf will make a tight fit around the reveal. Use a hand saw to cut out the shape of the reveal from the back corner of the shelf. Sand off any rough edges with fine-grade abrasive paper and a sanding block.

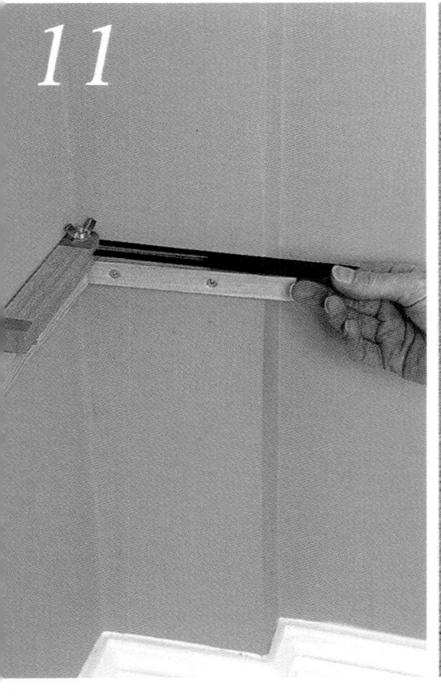

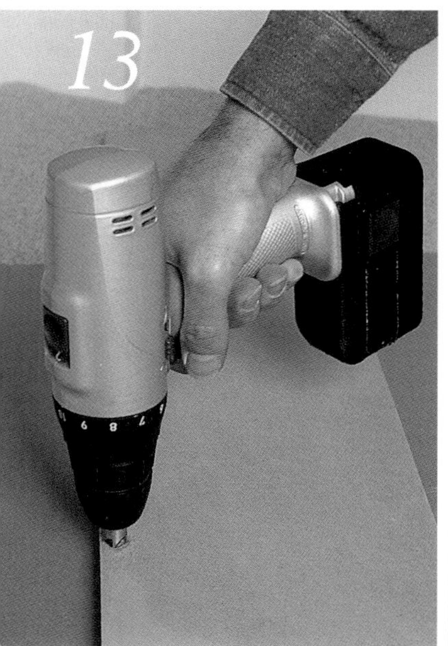

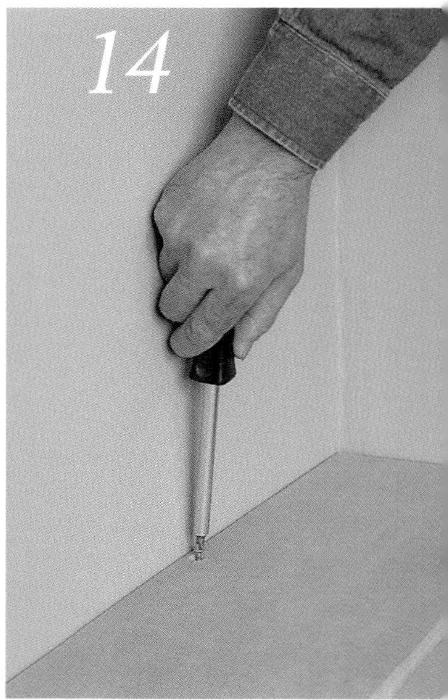

13 Hold the shelf up against the battens and check that it fits neatly both into the alcove and around any reveal. Make any adjustments to the fit as necessary. Use a ⅙ in. bit to drill evenly spaced fixing holes through the shelf and into the tops of the battens. Countersink the holes.

14 Use a hand screwdriver to attach the shelf to the wall battens using No. 6 (1½ in.) screws. Do not be tempted to try and speed things up by using the power drill and screwdriver bit—if you do this, you will almost certainly damage the wall decor behind the shelf.

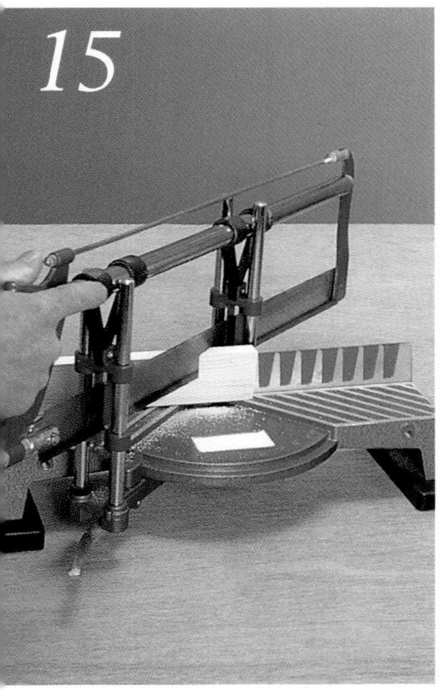

15 Take the edging strip and hold it up against the shelf. Mark off the positions for miters at each end of the edging strip. Use a miter saw to cut 45-degree miters into each end of the edging strip. Measure and miter small pieces of edging to cover the protruding side edges of the shelf.

16 Secure the edging strip to the front and side edges of the shelf using a thin layer of wood glue and evenly spaced 1 in. panel pins. Fill, sand, and paint or varnish the shelf as you wish.

building a display case

If you are a collector of ornaments, or any other small items, you will know about the storage problems that go with your hobby. Create a showcase for your hobby that will increase the pleasure your pastime brings even more.

Materials (all lumber is softwood unless otherwise stated)

Top: 1 piece of lumber 1 x 3¾ x 14 in.

Bottom: 1 piece of lumber 1 x 3¾ x 14 in.

Back: 1 piece of plywood ¼ x 15½ x 22 in.

Sides: 2 pieces of lumber 1 x 3¾ x 22 in.

Shelves: 5 or more glass shelves 3¾ x 14 in.

Shelf supports: 20 pieces of lumber ¼ x ¼ x 3¾ in.

Door: 2 pieces of lumber 1 x 1 x 16 in.; 2 pieces of lumber 1 x 1 x 22 in.

Door facing: 2 pieces of mitered lumber ¼ x 1½ x 16 in.; 2 pieces of mitered lumber ¼ x 1½ x 22 in.

1 sheet of glass 15 x 21 in. • 2 brass hinges • 1 brass door catch • No. 6 (2 in.) screws • 1 in. panel pins • Wood glue • Wood filler

Tools

Workbench • Power drill with ¼ in., ⅙ in., screw, and countersinking bits • Hammer • Bradawl • Tape measure • Rule • Carpenter's pencil • Filling knife • Fine-grade abrasive paper/sanding block

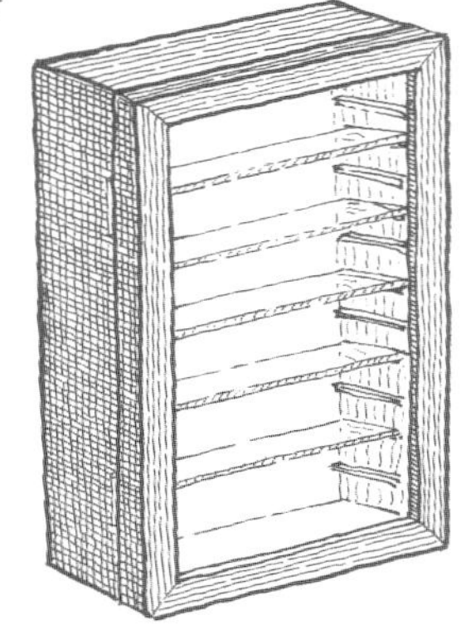

Skill level

Intermediate

Time

8 hours

1 Measure and cut all the pieces to the dimensions given in the list of materials. Lay the two side pieces on the workbench. Use a combination square and pencil to mark the position of the butt joints for the adjoining top and bottom pieces at each end. These should be drawn across the side pieces to the thickness of the top and bottom pieces (1 in.) Next, mark the positions of the shelf supports on the side pieces. There are ten shelf supports for each side piece. The supports should be positioned at least 1 in. apart from each other, starting 3 in. up from the bottom edge of the side pieces.

2 Take the twenty shelf supports and glue and pin them between their guidelines on the inside of the side pieces. Apply a thin layer of wood glue to each one and then hammer in two evenly spaced 1 in. panel pins to secure them to the sides.

3 Next, drill two evenly spaced ¼ in. clearance holes into the butt joint guidelines marked in step 1 at each end of the side pieces. These will take the screws that will attach the side pieces to the top and bottom of the display case. Lay a piece of scrap wood underneath the side pieces as you drill, to prevent making holes in the workbench.

4 Turn the side pieces over on the workbench so that the attached shelf supports are facing downward. Countersink the holes that you drilled in step 3.

5 Lay the two side pieces on their sides on the workbench. Hold the top and bottom pieces in position against the ends of the side pieces, so that their ends butt squarely together. Use a combination square to ensure that the pieces are properly square with each other. Drill 1/6 in. reciprocal pilot holes into the sides of the top and bottom pieces through the clearance holes that you drilled into the ends of the side pieces in step 3.

6 When you have drilled pilot holes into both ends of the top and bottom pieces, apply a thin layer of glue to each butt joint and secure the pieces with No. 6 (2 in.) screws. Use a hand screwdriver to drive in the screws, to ensure precision and control as you make the joints.

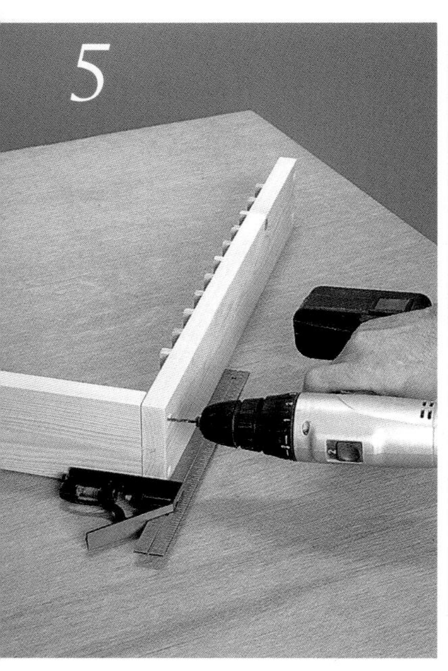

7 Once the basic carcass of the display case has been assembled, attach the back piece by hammering in four evenly spaced 1 in. panel pins along each long edge and three across the shorter top and bottom edges.

8 The next step is to begin assembling the door frame of the display case. Take the four pieces of the door frame and make butt joints at each end using the method described in step 6. Again, use a hand screwdriver to drive in the screws fixing the door frame pieces together, to ensure precision and good control as you make the butt joints.

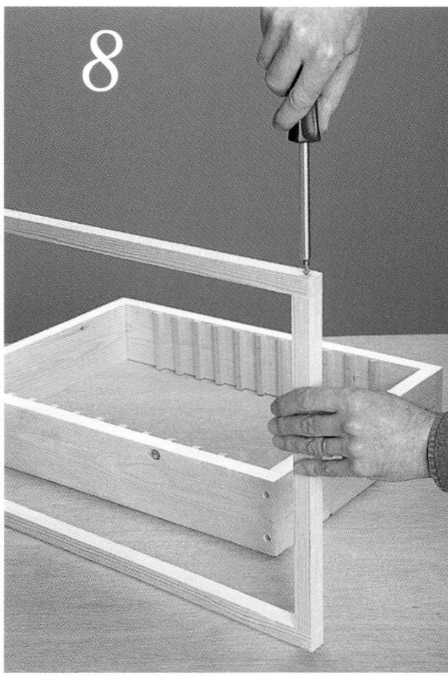

9 The door of the display case features a decorative facing with mitered joints that will disguise the basic butt joints that hold the door together. Hold up each length of facing to the door frame in turn and mark off miter cuts at their ends where the facing meets the end of the frame.

10 Use a miter saw to cut 45-degree miters into the ends of each of the four pieces of door facing. Sand off any rough edges to a smooth finish using fine-grade abrasive paper and a sanding block.

11 Hold the mitered lengths of door facing in position against the door frame in turn, so that their outside edges are level with the outside edges of the frame. The inner edges of the facing pieces will then overhang the inner edges of the door frame by approximately ¼ in., creating a "lip" all the way around the frame into which the glass pane of the door will fit. Attach the facing pieces to the door frame with a thin layer of wood glue and four evenly spaced 1 in. panel pins along each side.

12 Turn the frame over on the workbench and place the glass pane in position in it so that the glass rests on the "lip" created in step 11. Secure the glass by gently hammering in four evenly spaced 1 in. panel pins along each side of the frame, just behind the glass. Turn the door over and repeat on the other side (as shown).

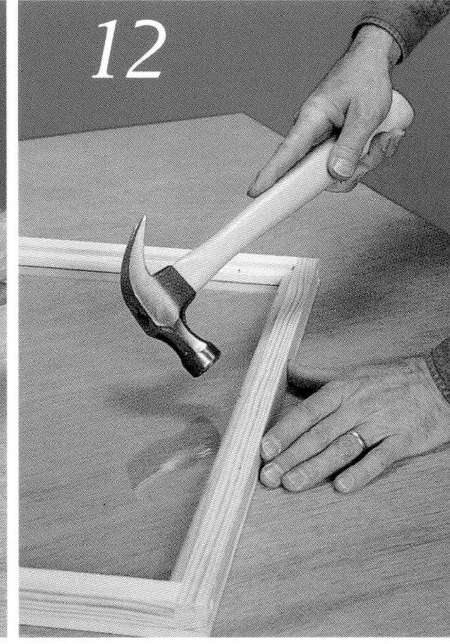

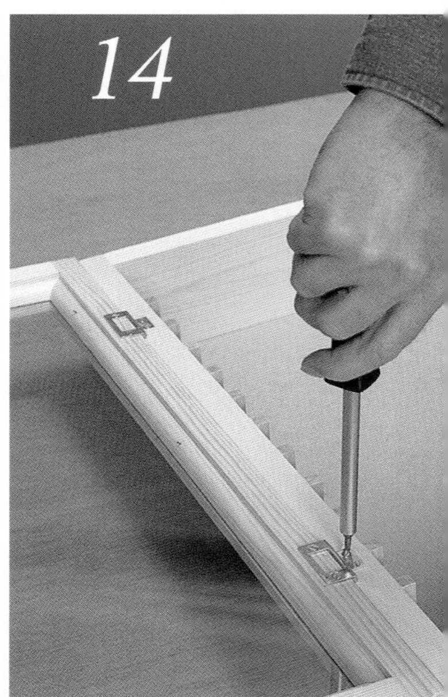

13 Take the two brass hinges and mark their fixing positions on the inside back edge of the door frame, 6 in. from each end. Use a bradawl to mark fixing points on the frame through the screw holes in the hinges. Attach the hinges to the door frame using the screws that should have been supplied with the hinges.

14 Lay the carcass of the display case face upward on the workbench. Lay the door down alongside the case so that it lines up accurately at the top and bottom. Once you are satisfied that the door is in the correct position, attach the other sides of the door hinges to the display case frame, in the same way as you did in step 13.

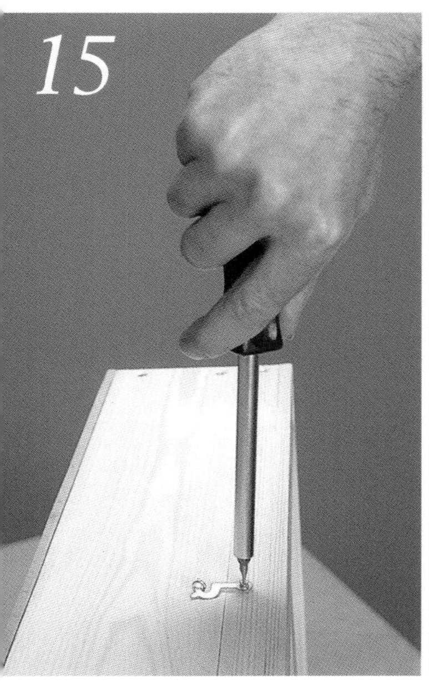

5 Mark the fixing position for the door catch at the center point of the right-hand outside edge, where the door will meet the display case when it is closed. Secure the door catch to the outside of the display case as shown, following the manufacturer's instructions. Fix the reciprocal part of the catch to the door itself. Fill, sand, and brush off the display case as necessary, being careful not to break the glass door.

6 Complete the display case by sliding the glass shelves into position between the shelf supports that you attached in step 2. Position the shelves at whichever heights suit the objects you wish to display.

chapter 2
Furniture

making a **magazine rack**

This magazine rack follows a traditional English design known as the "Canterbury," and will bring a stylish touch to any living room. The unit will hold approximately ten magazines. It is not difficult to make, and looks good in bare wood. When constructing the rack, concentrate on sound, tight joints and bringing a smooth finish to the wood.

Materials (all lumber is softwood unless otherwise stated)

Bottom: 1 piece of MDF ½ x 4 x 15½ in.

Ends: 2 pieces of MDF ½ x 10 x 15 in.

Sides: 2 pieces of MDF ½ x 11 x 15½ in.

Handles: 2 pieces of oak ⅜ x ⅝ x 10 in.

No. 6 (1½ in.) brass screws and screw cups • Wood filler • Small can of varnish

Tools

Workbench • Rule • Combination square • Carpenter's pencil • Power drill with ⅙ in., ⅛ in., screw, and countersinking bits • Hand screwdriver • Fine-grade abrasive paper/sanding block • Paint brush • Soft brush

Skill level

Beginner

Time

4 hours

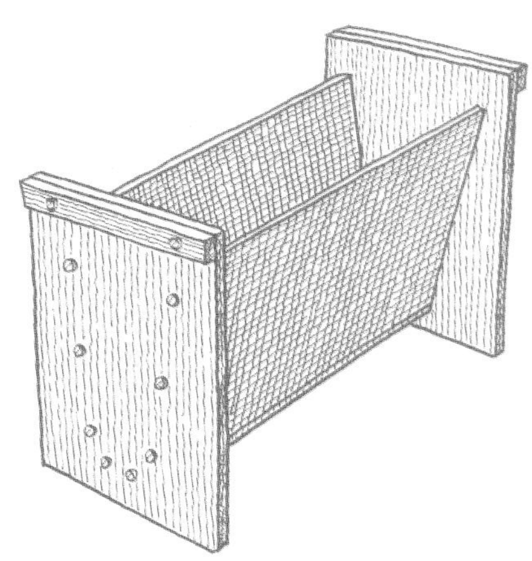

1 Lay the end pieces flat on the workbench and use a combination square and pencil to mark out the fixing positions of the sides and bottom. Take one end piece and mark a central point across its width, 3 in. up from its bottom edge. Draw a line, 4 in. long, centered at this point. Draw a parallel line 4½ in. long centered above the first line. Measure 1 in. in from the top corners of the end piece. Draw a line from each point, connecting it to the end of the lowest horizontal line. Measure ¾ in. in from the marks you have made on the top edge, and join these points to each end of the other horizontal line.

2 Turn the end pieces over on the workbench and mark the fixing positions of the two oak handles at their top ends, as shown. The handles should butt squarely with the top and side edges of the end pieces as you draw the fixing guidelines along them.

1

2

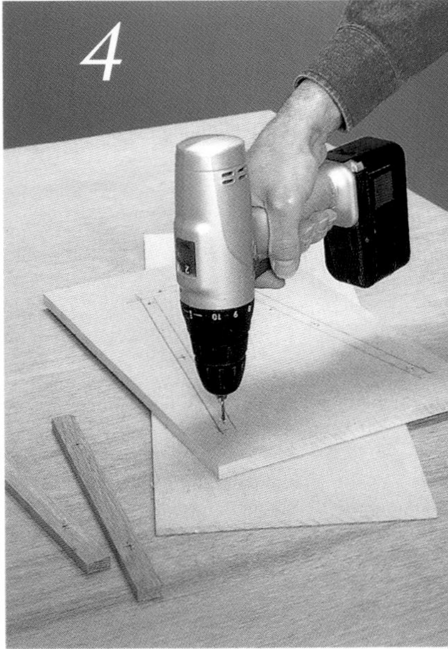

3 Turn the end pieces over again so that their insides and the side piece fixing guidelines are facing upward. Mark evenly spaced fixing points for screws along the guidelines, two for the bottom piece and three each for the sides.

4 Use a ⅙ in. bit to drill clearance screw holes at the points you marked in step 3. Place a piece of scrap wood under the end pieces as you drill, to prevent making holes in the workbench.

Helpful hints

If you want to increase the size of your magazine rack, use a wider bottom piece and adjust the angles of the two side pieces accordingly to take more magazines.

5 The next step is to attach the bottom piece to the two end pieces. Turn the end pieces upside down and clamp them onto the edge of the workbench in turn, as shown, so that the bottom piece fixing guidelines that you marked in step 1 align with the top of the work surface. Place the bottom piece in position so that its end butts up squarely with the fixing guidelines marked on the inside of the end piece. Use a ⅛ in. bit to drill pilot holes into the end of the bottom piece through the clearance holes that you drilled in the end piece in step 4. Repeat with the other end piece at the opposite end of the bottom piece.

6 Use No. 6 (1½ in.) brass screws and screw cups to attach the end pieces to the bottom piece through the holes that you drilled in steps 4 and 5.

7 Repeat the process described in steps 5 and 6 to attach the sides of the rack to the two end pieces. Again, use No. 6 (1½ in.) brass screws and screw cups to make the joints. The cups will recess the heads of the screws and also make an attractive design feature. Next, attach the two oak handles to the top outside edges of the end pieces (as shown), again using No. 6 (1½ in.) brass screws and screw cups to make the joints.

8 Fill and sand the magazine rack as necessary, paying particular attention to the joints. Brush off the unit and finish by painting it with either matte or gloss varnish, according to your preference.

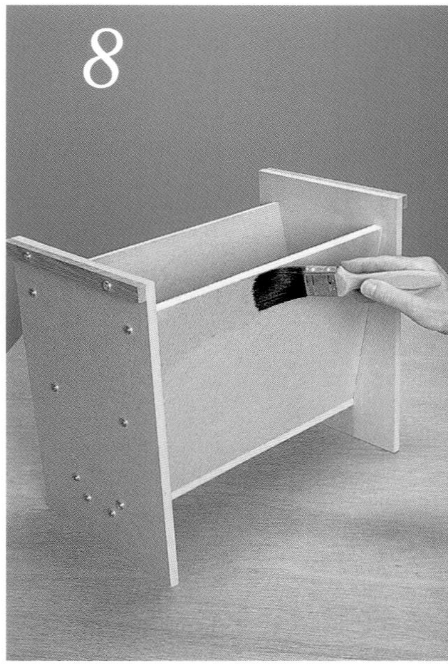

making an **occasional table**

This "occasional" table both looks good and offers practical versatility, featuring a useful shelf for storage. It is handy and convenient for all kinds of different purposes, and elegant at the same time.

Materials (all lumber is softwood unless otherwise stated)

Table top: 1 piece of MDF 1 x 16 x 48 in.

Shelf: 1 piece of MDF ½ x 14 x 45½ in.

Legs: 4 pieces of PAR 2 x 2 x 16 in.

Side facing pieces: 2 pieces of PAR ¼ x 1¼ x 48½ in.

End facing pieces: 2 pieces of PAR ¼ x 1¼ x 16½ in.

Shelf side facing pieces: 2 pieces of PAR ¼ x 1¾ x 47 in.

Shelf end facing pieces: 2 pieces of PAR ¼ x 1¾ x 15½ in.

Side battens: 2 pieces of PAR 1 x 1 x 47 in.

2 in. panel pins • Wood glue • Wood filler • Small can of paint (your choice of color) • Small can of matte or gloss varnish

Tools

Workbench • Tenon saw • Miter saw • Tape measure • Set-square/combination square • Carpenter's pencil • Hammer • Nail punch • Rule • Fine-grade abrasive paper/ sanding block • Brush or soft cloth • Paint brushes

Skill level

Intermediate

Time

4 hours

1 The first stage is to draw out the fixing guidelines and general assembly plan for the table on the underside of the table top. Take the table top and lay it flat on the workbench, with the underside facing upward. Hold the side- and end-facing pieces in position along the sides and ends of the table top and draw along their edges. Next, lay the shelf on the table top, ensuring that it is positioned centrally, and draw around its edge. Then, hold one of the table legs in position at one corner of the shelf guidelines and draw around its end to mark its fixing position, as shown. Repeat at all four corners.

2 Place the shelf in position on the table top and mark the fixing positions of the four legs onto its corners, in the same way that you marked the underside of the table top in step 1.

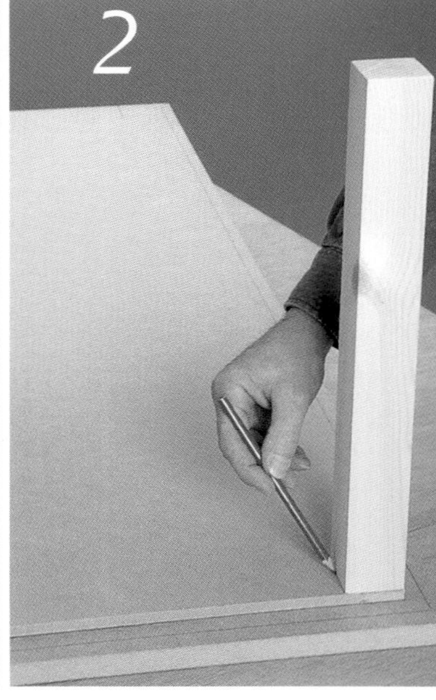

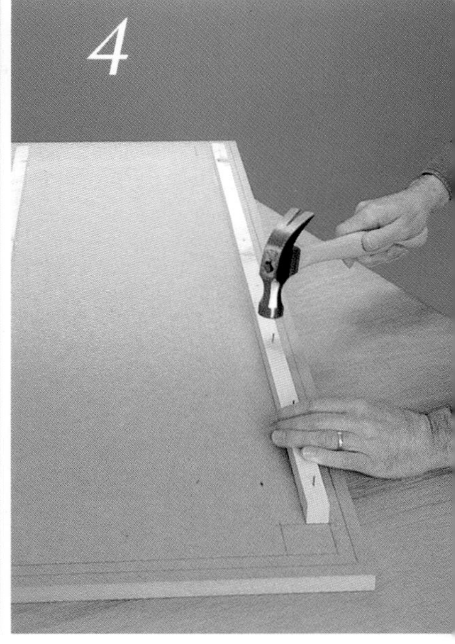

3 When you have marked the positions of the four legs onto the shelf, remove the table top from beneath it and clamp the shelf to the workbench. Use a tenon saw to cut out the rebates for the four legs. Sand off any rough edges using fine-grade abrasive paper and a sanding block.

4 Place the table top face down on the workbench. Take the two side battens and position them along each side of the table top, aligned with the guidelines you drew along the side facing pieces in step 1. The ends of the battens will align with the inside leg fixing guidelines that were also marked in step 1. Apply a thin layer of glue to the underside of each batten. Then, starting at one end of each batten, hammer eight evenly spaced panel pins along their lengths to secure them to the underside of the table top.

5 Take the two side-facing pieces and hold them up against the attached battens on the underside of the table top. Butt a combination square up against the end of the battens and the sides of the facing pieces. Use a pencil to mark miter joints at each end of the facing pieces where they meet the ends of the battens, as shown.

6 Use a miter saw to cut the miters at each end of the two side facing pieces. Sand off any rough edges using fine-grade abrasive paper and a sanding block.

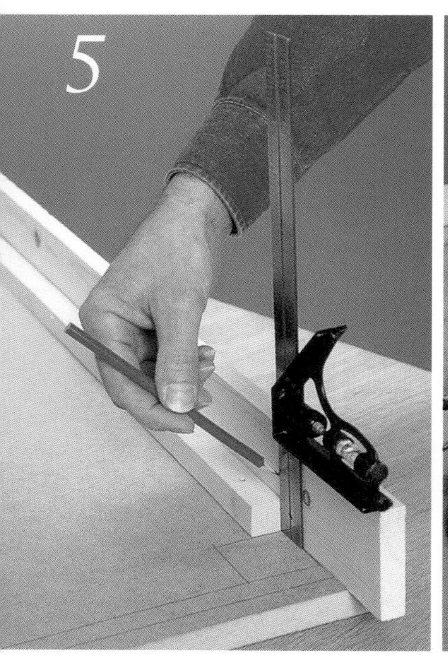

7 The next stage is to attach the side-facing pieces to the tops of the table legs. Lay two of the legs at a time on the workbench and place one of the side-facing pieces in position over the legs, so that the top and end edges of the facing pieces align squarely with the top and back edges of the table legs. Use a combination square to check that the pieces are squarely aligned, as shown. Hammer two vertically and evenly spaced panel pins through the ends of the side-facing piece to attach it to the two legs. Repeat the process with the other two legs and side-facing piece.

8 Next, attach the two longer shelf-facing pieces to the legs using the same method as described in step 7. These should be positioned with their top edges 6 in. up from the bottoms of the legs. Use a nail punch to recess all the panel pins.

9 Place the table top on the workbench with the underside and attached battens facing upward. Hold one of the sets of legs and facing pieces in position on the table top, so that the legs sit in their marked positions with their inner sides butting against the ends of the batten. Apply a thin layer of glue along the inside edge of the side-fixing piece where it butts with the batten. Starting at one end of the facing piece just inside the first leg, hammer eight evenly spaced panel pins along its length until it is firmly attached to the batten. Repeat with the other set of legs and side fixing piece.

10 Attach the shelf to the two long shelf facing pieces using the same method as described in step 9. Ensure that the top side of the shelf aligns perfectly with the top edge of the shelf facing pieces before hammering in the panel pins.

11 The next stage is to attach the two shorter, end shelf-facing pieces to the shelf. Follow the method described in steps 5 and 6 to mark and cut miters for the ends of the two pieces. This will ensure neat, tidy joints when they are attached to the shelf and the table legs.

12 Glue and pin the two shorter shelf-facing pieces to the ends of the shelf, following the method described in step 9. Use four panel pins for each shelf end facing piece, ensuring that one is hammered firmly into each leg to help strengthen the table. If any glue squeezes out of your joints and onto the table top or other surface, wipe it off immediately with a damp cloth.

13 Follow the method described in steps 9, 11, and 12 to attach the two end facing pieces to the table top. Ensure that the top edges of the facing pieces align perfectly with the table top and adjoining side-facing pieces before hammering in the panel pins. Again, use four panel pins for each end-facing piece. Recess all the panel pin heads using a nail punch.

14 Use a filling knife and proprietary wood filler to fill all the panel pin holes and any gaps in the table. Check all your joints carefully and complete them smoothly with the wood filler as necessary.

15 Allow the wood filler to dry thoroughly and then use fine-grade abrasive paper and a sanding block to rub the table down all over to a smooth finish. Brush off filler and wood dust thoroughly with a soft cloth or brush.

16 Finally, varnish the table top, using matte or gloss varnish according to your preference. Paint the legs and shelf in a color that complements the varnished table top and the decor of your room. Allow to dry thoroughly, according to the manufacturer's instructions, and your occasional table is ready for use.

making a low-level **coffee table**

This low, rectangular table is an attractive centerpiece for any living room. The table can be constructed from simple MDF or either beech or ash—both attractive, hard-wearing woods—and consists of a two-tier, open-sided oblong box on large castors. Edged with strips of oak, it is elegant, portable, and practical.

Materials

Top: 1 piece of MDF ¾ x 18 x 36 in.

Bottom: 1 piece of MDF ¾ x 18 x 36 in.

Sides: 2 pieces of MDF ¾ x 18 x 8½ in.

Central upright divider: 1 piece of MDF ¾ x 15 x 8½ in.

Edging: 1 piece of oak ¾ in. x 18 ft.

Battens: 2 pieces 1 x 1 in. PAR timber

No. 6 (1 in.) screws • No. 8 (1½ in.) brass screws and screw cups • 1 in. panel pins • Wood glue • 4 x 4 in.-deep castors

Tools

Workbench • Miter saw • Power drill with ⅙ in., ⅛ in., ¹⁄₁₆ in., and screw bits • Hammer • Nail punch • Abrasive paper/ sanding block

Skill level

Intermediate

Time

4 hours

1 Hold the side pieces up to the underside of the top piece and mark their positions on it at the ends, drawing pencil guidelines along the edges of the side pieces. Take the central upright divider piece and mark its position centrally on the top piece in the same way (as shown), 18 in. from each end and 1½ in. in from the front and back edges.

2 Take the two 1 x 1 in. PAR battens and mark their positions each side of the guidelines for the central upright divider. These will hold the divider in place on the underside of the coffee table top. Drill three evenly spaced clearance holes through each batten using an ⅛ in. drill bit. Drill reciprocal pilot holes through the clearance holes into the top piece using a 1⁄16 in. drill bit. Use No. 6 (1 in.) screws to attach the battens to the top piece, as shown.

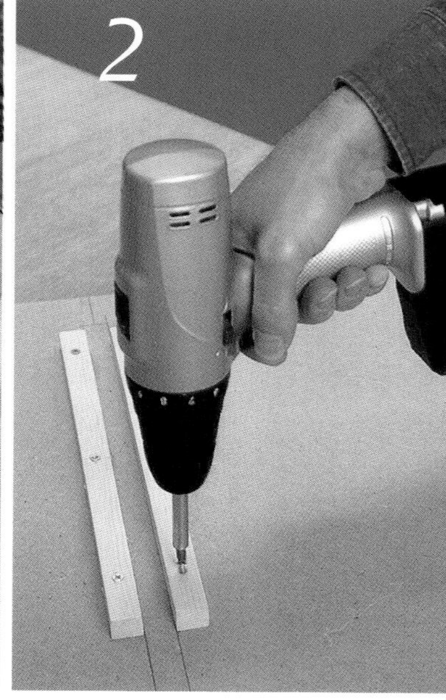

3 Mark and drill three ⅛ in. evenly spaced clearance holes in the centers of the side piece guidelines that you drew on the top piece in step 1. Take the bottom piece and butt it alongside the top piece on the workbench. Transpose all the guidelines and fixing hole marks from the top piece to the bottom piece. Drill identical clearance holes in the bottom piece, and three additional ones in the guidelines for the central upright divider piece.

4 Hold the side pieces against the bottom piece on the workbench. Ensure that the pieces are butted squarely together. Drill reciprocal pilot holes into the edges of the side pieces through the clearance holes that you drilled in the bottom piece in step 3. Attach the bottom piece to the two side pieces using No. 8 (1½ in.) brass screws and screw cups.

5 Place the top piece on the workbench with its underside facing upward. Slide the central upright divider into position between the two battens that you attached to the top piece in step 2. Place the bottom piece and attached sides carefully in position over the central divider and top piece. Drill ⅛ in. pilot holes into the divider through the clearance holes in the bottom piece. Attach the central upright divider to the bottom piece using No. 8 (1½ in.) brass screws and screw cups.

6 Turn the unit over on the workbench and remove the top piece. Turn it over so that the attached battens are facing upward. Apply wood glue sparingly in the gap between the battens. This is to help secure the central upright divider and means you do not need to drive screws through the middle of the coffee table surface.

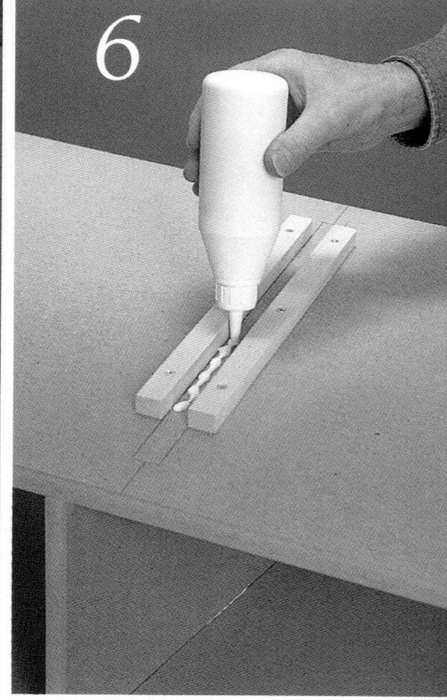

7 Turn the top piece over and press it carefully into position over the central upright divider and the rest of the unit. Wipe off any glue that squeezes out from between the battens using a damp cloth. As before, drill reciprocal ⅛ in. pilot holes into the sides through the clearance holes in the edges of the top piece. Attach the top piece to the sides of the table using No. 8 (1½ in.) brass screws and screw cups.

8 Cut a piece of oak edging to a length 2 in. longer than the assembled unit. Hold the edging piece up to the front of the coffee table. Mark 45-degree miter joint cuts in the oak edging piece at each end of the unit, where the top piece joins the sides.

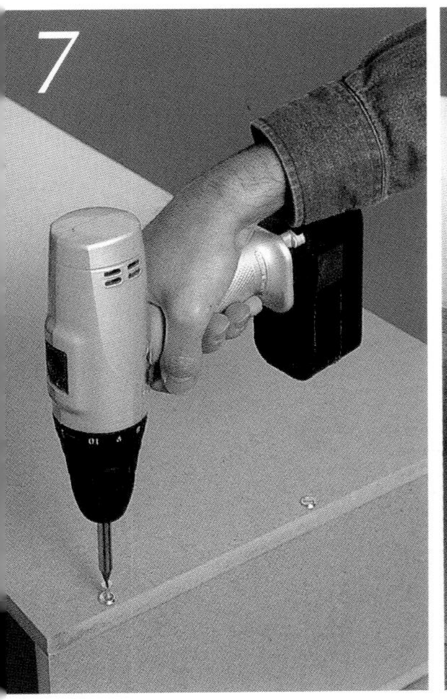

9 Use a miter saw to cut 45-degree miters on each end of the oak edging piece for the front edge of the coffee table. Sand off any rough edges using a block and medium-grade abrasive paper. Repeat steps 8 and 9 for the oak edging strips to be attached to the front edges of the sides, bottom piece, and the central upright divider.

10 Hammer evenly spaced 1 in. panel pins halfway into the edging strips to fit on the front of the coffee table, using five pins for the long edges and two for the sides and central upright divider pieces. Apply a thin layer of wood glue to each of the front edges of the coffee table. Then, fix the edging strips firmly to the unit, nailing the panel pins all the way into the strips. Use a nail punch to recess the pin heads. Turn the unit over and repeat steps 8–10 for the back of the table.

1 Turn the coffee table upside down on the workbench. Take the four castors to be fitted to the bottom of the unit. Mark the position of each one in turn, at the four corners of the unit. Ensure that the castor wheels will not protrude from the edges of the coffee table by swivelling them around as you hold them in position. Drill fixing holes through the castor bracket holes, using a drill bit that matches the size of your castors' holes.

2 Attach the four castors to the underside of the coffee table following the manufacturer's instructions. Most castors will need to be bolted to the table, as shown. Fill, sand, and varnish the table, according to your preference.

making a **footstool**

This upholstered footstool is big enough to sit on and low enough to put your feet up on. It also provides useful storage space, as it has a hollow base. Choose the upholstery fabric to match your living room decor.

Materials (all lumber is softwood unless otherwise stated)

Seat: 1 piece of foam 4 x 14 x 32 in; 2 pieces of fabric 36 x 48 in. • **Seat base:** 2 pieces of ply ¼ x 13½ x 31½ in. • **Bottom:** 1 piece of MDF 1 x 15 x 33 in. • **Front and back:** 2 pieces of MDF ½ x 14 x 33 in. • **Sides:** 2 pieces of MDF 1 x 14 x 15 in. • **Upright battens:** 4 pieces of lumber 1½ x 1½ x 11 in. • **Top battens:** 2 pieces of lumber 1 x 2 x 10 in.; 2 pieces of lumber 1 x 2 x 28 in. • **Top edging:** 2 pieces of lumber ½ x ½ x 15 in.; 2 pieces of lumber ½ x ½ x 33 in. • **Plinth:** 2 pieces of lumber ½ x 1¾ x 16 in.; 2 pieces of lumber ½ x 1¾ x 34 in. • **Feet:** 4 pieces of lumber 1 x 1¾ x 1¾ in. • No. 6 (1½ in.) screws • 2 in. panel pins • Wood glue • Wood filler • Double-sided tape

Tools

Workbench • Miter saw • Power drill with ½ in., ⅛ in., screw, and countersinking bits • Staple gun • Hammer • Nail punch • Tape measure • Rule • Carpenter's pencil • Filling knife • Fine-grade abrasive paper/sanding block

Skill level

Intermediate

Time

8 hours

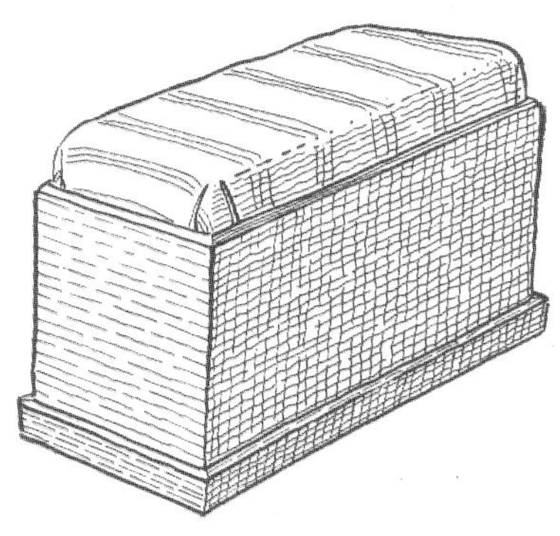

1 The first step is to mark out the internal batten framework of the footstool. The upright battens strengthen the footstool and the top battens create the recess for the seat. Place the front and back pieces on the workbench and mark out the positions of the upright and top battens on their insides. Butt the upright battens against the ends of these pieces, drawing along their inner side and bottom edges as shown, leaving ½ in. between the bottom end of the batten and the bottom edge of the panel, and ½ in. between the outside edge of the batten and the edge of the panel. Then, hold the long top battens in position above your marks for the uprights and draw a line along their bottom edges to mark their fixing positions.

2 Take the two side pieces and draw the same frame pattern on them as in step 1. Ensure that your marks line up perfectly with those drawn on the side pieces.

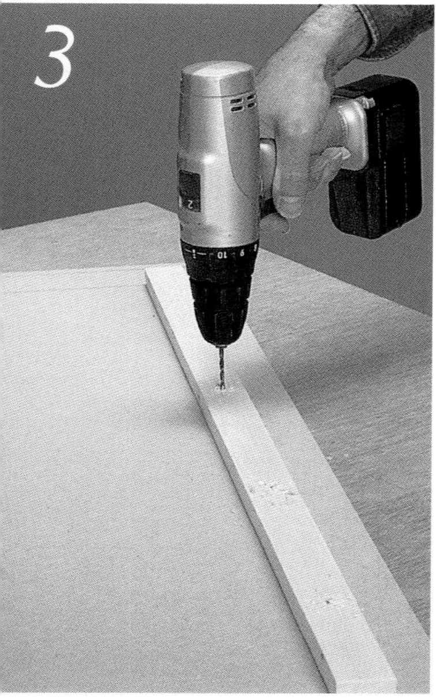

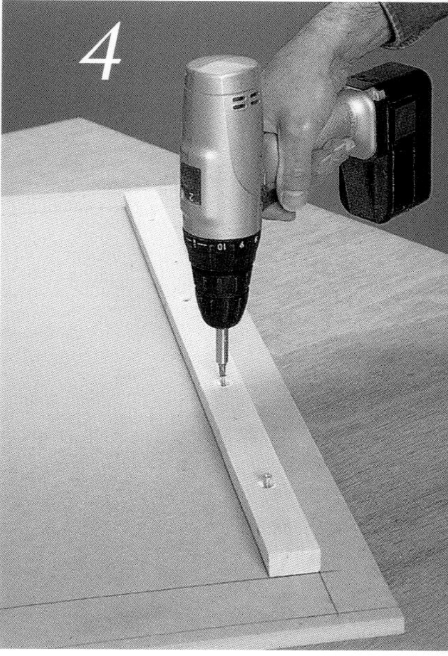

3 Place the two long top battens in position along their fixing guidelines on the front and back pieces, ensuring that their ends butt with the fixing guidelines for the upright battens at each end. Starting at one end of the long battens, drill five evenly spaced ⅛ in. pilot holes through each batten and into the front and back. Be sure that you set your drill bit to a depth to prevent you from drilling all the way through to the "good" side of the panels. Countersink all the screw holes.

4 Attach the two long top battens to the side pieces using a thin layer of wood glue and No. 6 (1½ in.) screws.

5 Drill three evenly spaced ⅛ in. clearance holes for each upright batten in the fixing guidelines on the inside of the front and back panels. Slightly offset the screw positions, so that they will not clash with those of the screws that will secure the end pieces to the upright battens when the carcass of the footstool is assembled.

6 Turn the front and back panels over on the workbench and countersink the clearance holes that you drilled in step 5. The screws for the carcass assembly will be driven in from the outside of the footstool. Attach the upright battens to the side pieces from their external sides, using the method described in step 4.

7 Stand or clamp the front and back panels upright on the workbench and hold the end pieces in position up against them. The end pieces must butt squarely with the upright battens, to which they will be attached, and the edges of the end and side pieces should also be completely square with each other. Drill three evenly spaced $\frac{1}{6}$ in. pilot holes into each of the upright battens through the end pieces. Countersink the holes and attach the end pieces to the upright battens using a little wood glue and No. 6 ($1\frac{1}{2}$ in.) screws, as in step 4.

8 Once the carcass of the footstool has been assembled, the next step is to prepare and attach the plinth at the bottom. Hold each of the plinth pieces up against the carcass in turn and mark miters at each end. Use a miter saw to cut 45-degree miters into the ends of the pieces.

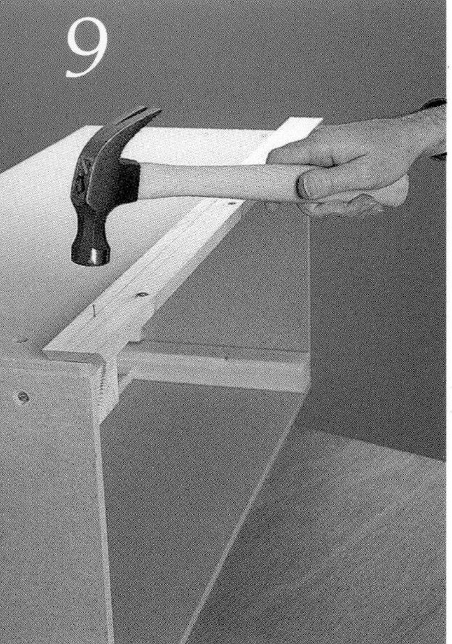

9 Lay the footstool carcass on its side on the workbench. Place the mitered plinth pieces in position along its length and at each end, in turn, ensuring that they overhang the bottom edge of the carcass by ½ in. Apply a thin layer of wood glue to each of the plinth pieces and secure them to the carcass with six evenly spaced panel pins along each side and three at each end.

10 Take the top edging pieces and prepare them using the method described in step 8. Attach the top edging pieces to the top edge of the carcass, again using a little wood glue and panel pins. Use a nail punch to recess the heads of the pins used to attach both the plinth and the top edging.

11 Once the plinth and top edging have been fixed in place, complete the carcass by attaching its bottom and feet. Turn the footstool upside down on the workbench and use the method described in step 7 to attach the bottom piece. Use three No. 6 (1½ in.) screws across each end and six along each side. Next, place the feet pieces at all four corners. Position each foot 1 in. in from the plinth on both sides. Drill a ⅛ in. pilot hole into the center of each foot and halfway through the thickness of the bottom piece. Attach the feet to the bottom using No. 6 (1½ in.) screws.

12 To prepare the seat of the footstool, place one of the plywood seat base pieces on the workbench. Attach a length of double-sided tape to each edge, as shown. Peel off the protective backing of the tape.

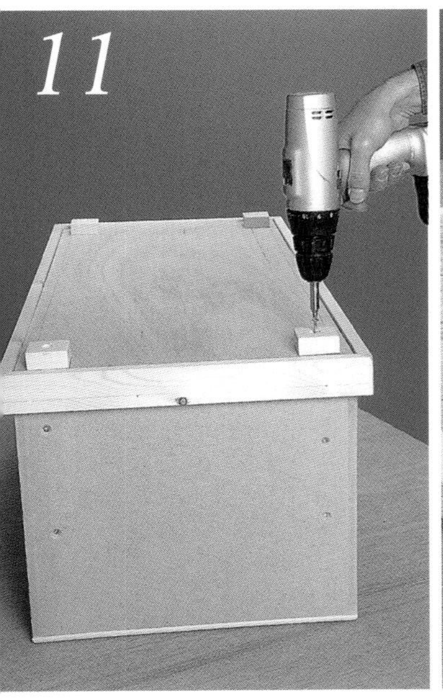

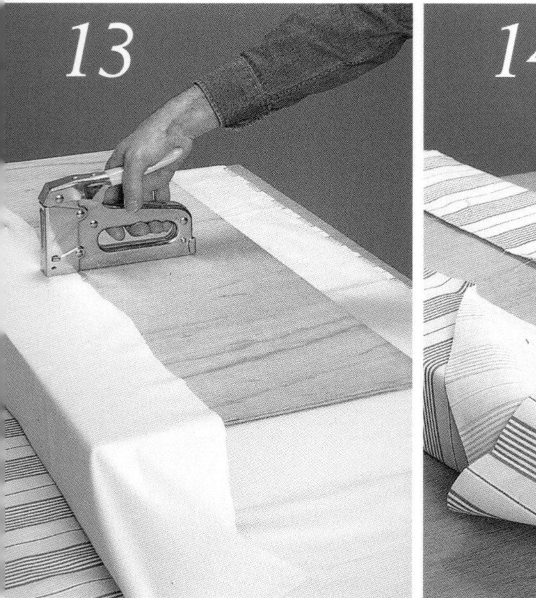

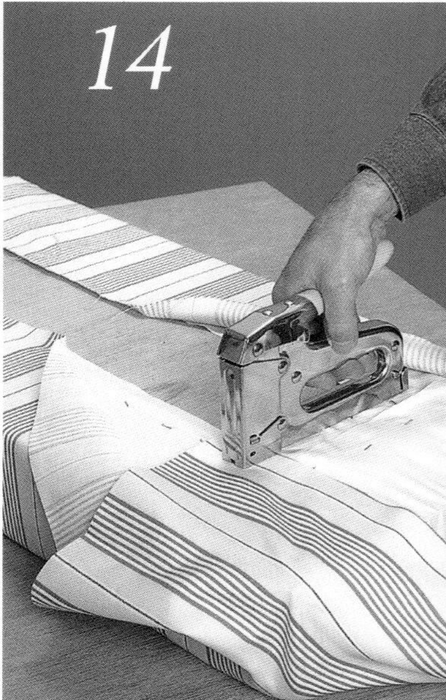

13 Take the piece of foam that makes up the padded seat, and stick it firmly onto the double-sided tape, ensuring that its edges are positioned squarely with those of the seat base. Lay the lining and covering fabrics out on the workbench. Place the foam seat and base onto the lining fabric, foam-side down. Wrap the lining fabric over the foam and seat base and begin attaching the fabric to the seat base using a staple gun. Fold the corners of the fabric into neat miters before also securing them with the staple gun.

14 When you have finished attaching the lining fabric to the seat, repeat the process with the covering fabric. Ensure that the fabric is tightly wrapped over the seat, with no creases.

5 Complete the upholstering of the seat by again making tightly mitered folds at each corner. Fold the long edge of the fabric up and over the mitered corners before punching in the staples, as shown. Be sure that the fabric is securely fastened at all points, using the staple gun to tighten up the fit where necessary.

6 Take the second plywood seat base piece and lay it over the first piece. Drive evenly spaced No. 6 (1½ in.) screws into the board all around its edge, using three screws along each side and one in the middle at each end. Secure the screws firmly through the first board and into the one underneath. Place the upholstered seat on the batten framework in the carcass, and your footstool is complete.

chapter **3**

Decoration

1. Hanging wallpaper

2. Fitting a dado rail and molding

3. Making tab-topped curtains

4. Putting up a wooden curtain pole

5. Making a cushion cover

hanging **wallpaper**

One of the quickest, easiest, and least expensive ways to transform your entire living room is to re-decorate the walls. Painting the walls is straightforward and relatively inexpensive, but with a little more money, time, and effort, you can enjoy the fulfilment of hanging your own personally selected wallpaper. There are few home improvements that can be more rewarding than hanging new wallpaper yourself, but you must be meticulous and take the time to do it properly, so that you do not have to live with bubbles or creases in your wallpaper.

Materials

Wallpaper • Lining paper (if required) • Wallpaper paste

Tools

Wallpapering table • Wallpapering brush • Wallpapering roller • Finishing brush • Tape measure • Plumb line • Scalpel/ hobby knife and spare blades • Large, sharp scissors • Bucket/bowl • Sponge • Low-tack adhesive tape

Skill level

Intermediate

Time

8 hours

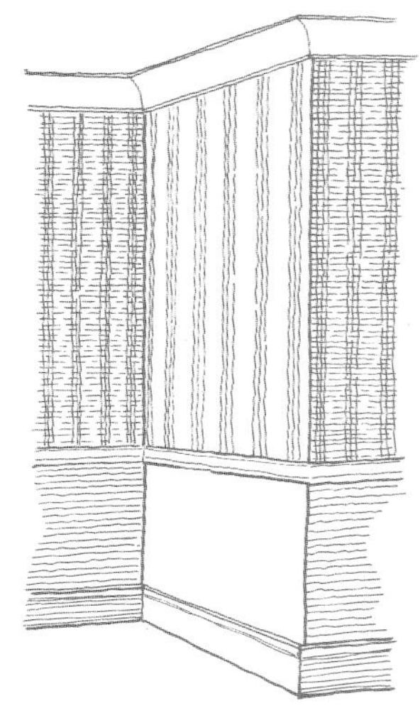

1 Measure the overall area that you wish to wallpaper and work out how many rolls of paper you will need in total. Lay the first roll of wallpaper out on a wallpapering table. Measure the length of drop for the first piece of paper, which will usually be from the ceiling to the dado rail or skirting board. Add 6 in. to your calculation and mark off the combined length on the first roll of paper. Cut the first piece of paper to length, using sharp scissors or a hobby knife and rule.

2 Prepare a bowl or bucket of wallpaper paste, carefully following the manufacturer's instructions. Thoroughly load up a wallpapering brush with paste and begin applying the paste to the length of wallpaper that you cut in step 1. Apply the paste from the center of the paper, out toward the edges.

1

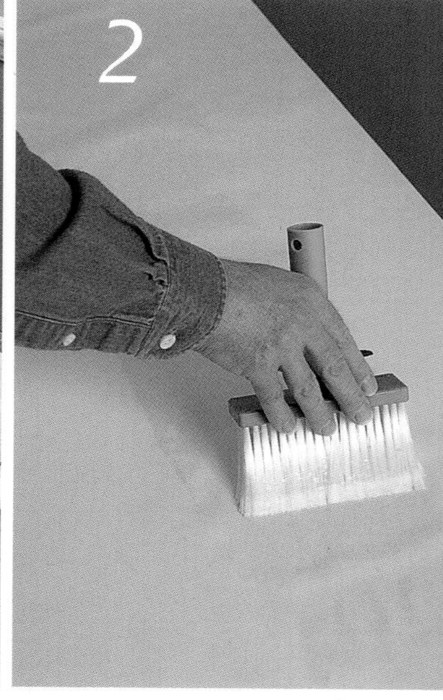
2

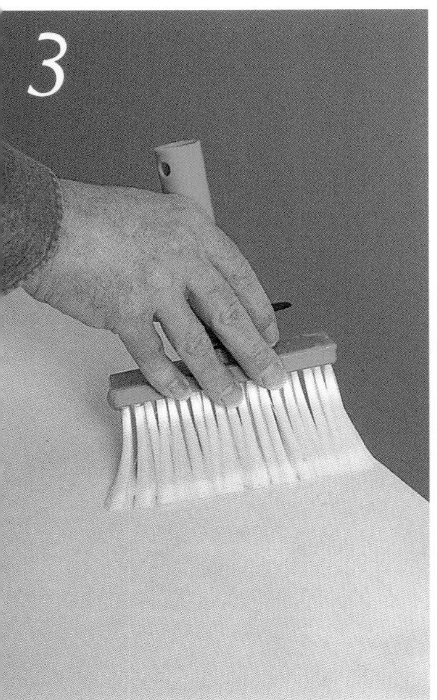

3 When the main part of the paper has been thoroughly coated in paste, carefully slide the wet paper across the table so that one of its long edges butts the edge of the table. Then, paste along the edge of the paper, ensuring that every part of it is lightly soaked in paste. Repeat on the other edge of the paper.

4 The next step is to begin attaching the paper to the wall. Always begin papering a wall from an internal corner. Measure the width of the paper less 1 in. from the internal corner. Hang a plumb line on the wall at this point (as shown), securing the top of the line with a piece of low-tack adhesive tape. The line will help you to hang the first piece straight and its position will allow for a 1 in. overlap of paper at the corner.

5 Return to the pasted length of paper lying on the wallpapering table. Fold a 3 in. overlap at each end of the piece of wallpaper. Then, fold the ends of the entire piece back over its rolled-out length until they meet in the middle, as shown. This makes the paper easier to handle as you lift it from the table.

6 Hold the wallpaper in position up against the wall, so that its right-hand edge butts with the plumb line that you attached in step 4, and its folded-over top edge butts with the top of the wall where it meets the ceiling. Gently unfurl the piece of wallpaper so that its entire length drops down the wall. Press the paper gently into place by hand. Then take a finishing brush and smooth out any air bubbles and creases, working the brush across the paper from the center outward.

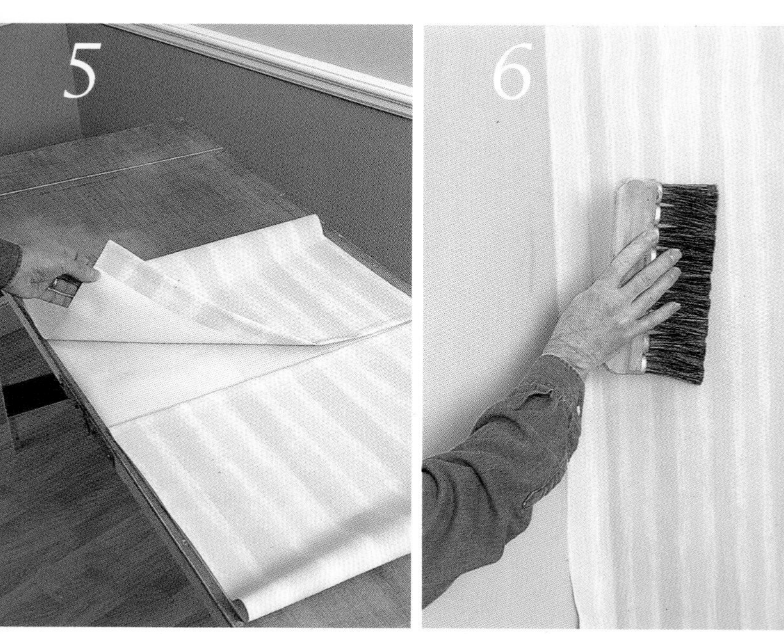

7 When you are satisfied with the position of the wallpaper and you have smoothed out any creases and air bubbles, allow the paste to dry for a little while, according to the manufacturer's instructions. Take a pair of scissors and run the blunt, backside of the blades along the edge of the paper at the point where the folded-over edge butts the ceiling or dado rail, as shown here. This will ensure that the paper is marked to a precise length before you cut off the excess, folded-over ends.

8 Before the paste dries out completely, gently peel a few inches of the paper away from its top or bottom edge and then cut away the excess, folded-over paper along the line marked with the back of the scissor blades in step 7.

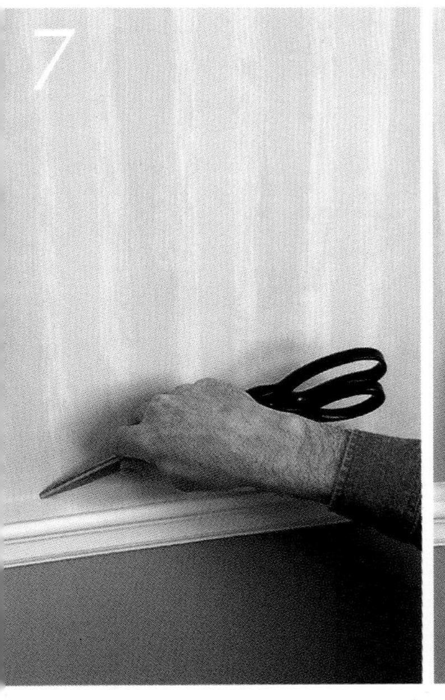

9 Use the finishing brush to ensure that the top and bottom edges of the paper are firmly stuck to the wall where it meets the ceiling, dado rail, and/or skirting board. Gently brush out any creases or air bubbles in the paper, as before. Repeat steps 7–9 along the edge of the paper where it meets the internal corner, cutting away the overlap so that the edge of the paper fits neatly into the corner.

10 Follow the procedure described in steps 1–9 for all pieces to be attached in the middle of a wall, but there is no need to allow for a corner overlap where a piece simply butts up against the last piece stuck to the wall. At an external corner, allow a 1 in. overlap and apply the edge around the corner, as shown. Then, cut and apply a 5 in.-wide strip for a neat join, butting the edge of the strip right up to the corner.

11 Use a wallpaper roller to secure the corner strip firmly over the edge of the piece that has been wrapped around the corner, pressing it tightly with the roller to disguise the joint between the two pieces as much as possible. The next full piece of wallpaper to be applied should be butted up against the edge of the corner strip.

12 Once you have pasted and cut all your pieces of wallpaper into place, finish off all the edges with a damp sponge. This will help the edges of the paper to stick firmly to the wall and will remove any excess paste that might have squeezed out from underneath the paper as you applied it to the wall.

fitting a dado rail **and molding**

Many modern homes lack the decorative, profiled moldings and dado rails that are a feature of some houses and which, today, still attract keen attention from prospective house-buyers. If your home falls into the former category, this project shows you how to bring about an impressive transformation to the walls of your living room. It is not difficult to fit traditional moldings and dado rails, and you can choose your own from a wide selection of designs, old and new.

Materials (all lumber is softwood unless otherwise stated)

Length of molding for top of base board (as per dimensions of your room) • Length of dado rail (as per dimensions of your room) • 2 in. panel pins • Wood glue • Wood filler • Tube of sealant

Tools

Workbench • Tenon saw • Miter saw • Tape measure • Rule • Spirit level • Set-square/combination square • Carpenter's pencil • Hammer • Nail punch • Rule • Sealant gun • Filling knife • Fine-grade abrasive paper/sanding block • Brush or soft cloth • Paint brushes • Sponge

Skill level

Beginner

Time

4 hours

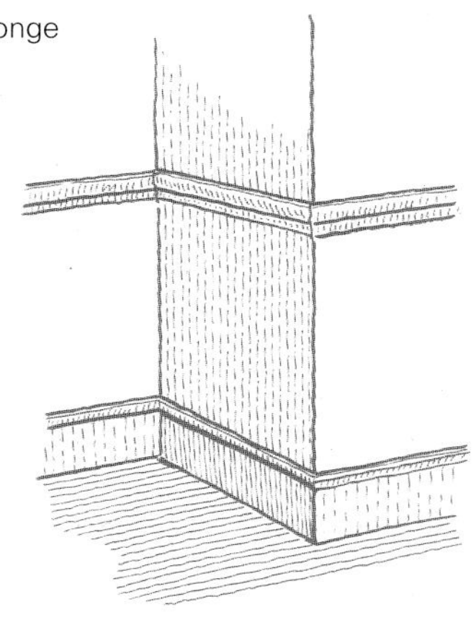

1 Begin by preparing the decorative molding to be attached to the top of your existing base board. Take the molding and, starting at an internal corner, measure off a length sufficient to cover the base board along one wall. Use a miter saw to cut a 45-degree miter into the end of the molding, so that it will fit neatly into the internal corner.

2 Hold the piece of molding in position, with its newly mitered corner flush with the top of the base board where it meets the internal corner of the wall. Mark off the position of the miter that will be required where the wall runs to its next corner, whether that be internal or external, as shown here. Cut a second miter in this end of the piece of molding.

3 Starting at one end of the prepared molding, hammer evenly spaced 2 in. panel pins part-way into the molding. Use one panel pin for every 12 in. of molding. Place the molding in position on top of the base board and begin hammering the panel pins all the way in. Use a piece of scrap card or paper propped up against the wall behind each panel pin to prevent you damaging the wall decor as you hammer in the pins. Fill and sand all the panel pin heads.

4 Take the tube of sealant and the sealant gun. Cut the nozzle of the tube to a width of approximately ¼ in., following the manufacturer's instructions. Then, draw a thin, smooth, bead of sealant steadily along the back edge of the molding where it meets the wall. Pull the nozzle of the gun along the joint as you make the bead, rather than pushing it. Wipe off any excess sealant.

5 The next step is to prepare and attach the dado rail. Use a rule, spirit level, and pencil to mark the fixing position of the dado rail on the wall. The top of a dado rail is normally positioned 36 in. up from the floor, but the height you choose is entirely up to you. Measure and mark your chosen height all the way around the walls to be railed, using the spirit level to ensure that your lines are straight. The dado rail needs to be mitered wherever it meets the corner of a wall. Measure and cut 45-degree miters in the ends of your dado rail following the procedure described for the decorative molding in step 1.

6 Dado rails have traditionally been stuck to the wall with glue rather than nails or panel pins, which could damage their moldings. Apply a thin layer of glue along the center of the piece of dado rail, as shown, prior to fixing it to the wall.

5

6

7 Press the dado rail into position on the wall, ensuring that it lines up perfectly with the pencil guideline that you drew in step 5. Run a spirit level along the dado rail to ensure that it is level. Wipe away any excess glue immediately with a damp cloth.

8 Follow steps 5–7 to measure, cut, and glue all the other pieces of dado rail into place. As far as possible, try and use one complete piece of dado rail per wall. Allow the glue to dry thoroughly and ensure that the dado rail is securely fastened to the wall. Then, fill the mitered corner joints as necessary and use fine-grade abrasive paper and a sanding block to bring them to a smooth finish. Paint or varnish as you wish.

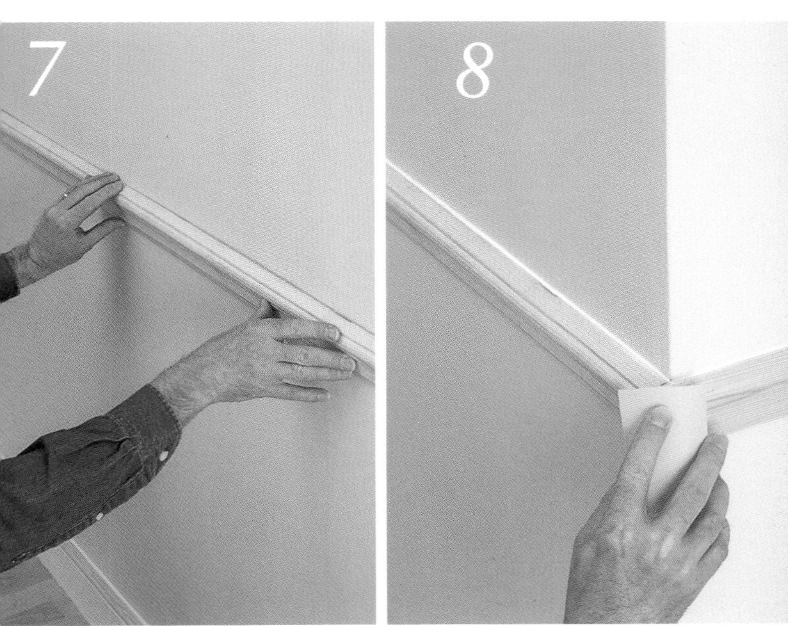

making tab-topped curtains

Good quality, lined curtains are a worthwhile addition to any living room. However, they are usually expensive to buy or have made—particularly if you want curtains that hang from ceiling to floor. These curtains, with their stylish loop attachments at the top, are easy to make and an inexpensive alternative to buying lined curtains.

Materials

Fabric to fit your window: Measure drop plus 8 in. and three-quarters of total width plus 4 in. for each curtain

Lining fabric: Actual size of drop and three-quarters of total width measurement for each curtain

Tab tops: 6 pieces of fabric 3 x 10 in. for each curtain

Stiffener fabric: 2 in. x 10 ft. length

Thread • Curtain rod

Tools

Worksurface • Electric sewing machine • Steam iron • Metal straightedge/rule • Scissors • Pins • Needle

Skill level

Intermediate

Time

4 hours

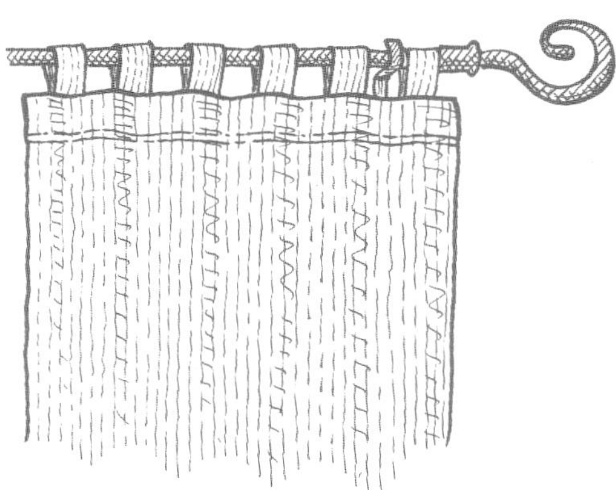

1 Cut all the pieces of fabric to the dimensions given in the list of materials. Take each piece of material for the curtain tabs and place them on the worksurface. Fold each tab piece in half lengthways. Then, fold the raw edges of the tab pieces over by ¼ in. Press all the folded tab edges thoroughly with a hot steam iron, as shown.

2 Cut a 2 in.-wide strip of stiffener fabric to the length of each folded curtain tab. Use a steam iron to iron the stiffening strips into the folded curtain tabs.

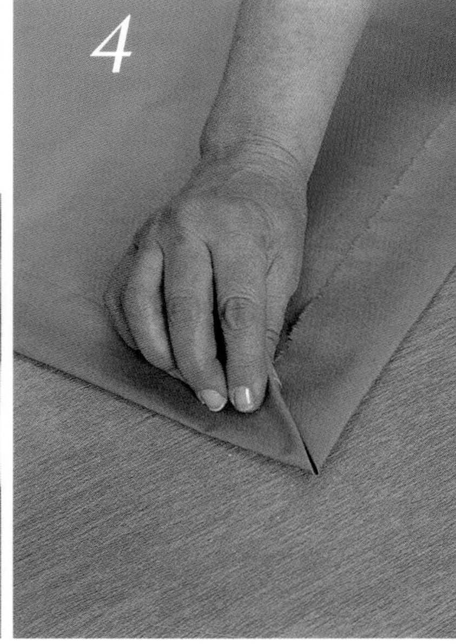

3 Machine stitch together the raw edges of the tabs about ¼ in. in from the edge of the fabric. Then sew a matching line of stitching inside the opposite, folded edge, as shown. Fold the tabs over in the middle so that they make loops.

4 Lay the curtain fabric face-down on the worksurface and fold in a 2 in. hem along both sides for each curtain. Pin the hem line all the way along each side and into neat, mitered corners at their ends. Do not fold a hem into the top end of the curtain fabric, as this is where the tabs will be fitted. Similarly, do not prepare the hem for the bottom end at this stage, as the curtains will need to be hung and checked for the correct length before the bottom hem can be positioned.

5 Take the curtain lining fabric and place it on the worksurface. Fold back a ½ in. hem along each side of the lining fabric for each curtain and press it into place with a hot steam iron.

6 Place the curtain fabric face down on the worksurface once more. Fold over a 2 in. hem all the way along the top end of the curtain fabric. Cut a length of 2 in.-wide stiffener fabric to fit into the fold that you have just made. Place the stiffening fabric into the fold, ensuring that it lies flat. Press the stiffening fabric thoroughly with a hot steam iron to bond it to the curtain fabric.

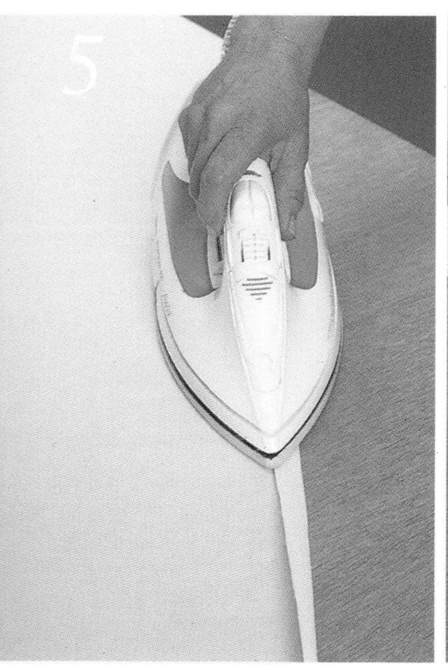

7 Take the stiffened, folded, and looped curtain tabs and pin them at evenly-spaced positions across the top end of the curtain. Use a rule to check on both the height and the positioning of the tabs as you pin them into place on the curtain.

8 Once you are completely satisfied with the spacing and positioning of the tabs, lay the lining fabric neatly over the top of the curtain so that it butts up to the folded hems along the sides of the curtain. Use pins along all four edges to secure the lining fabric to the curtain.

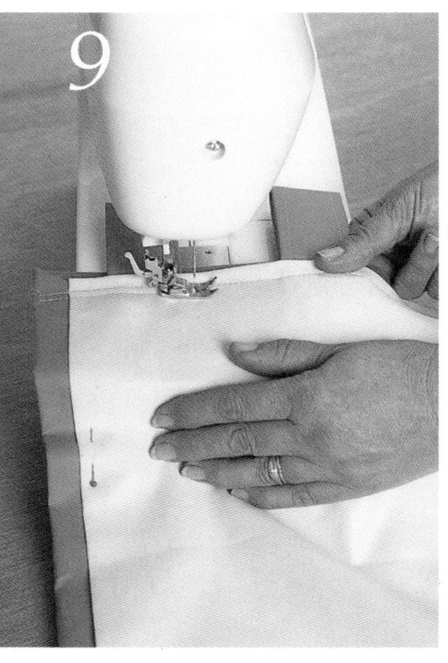

9 Use the electric sewing machine to sew a double row of stitching across the top of the curtain to secure the bottoms of the tabs in between the curtain and lining fabrics.

10 Slip stitch the lining fabric to the side folds of the curtain fabric. Ensure that the lining fabric is stitched straight along the sides of the curtain.

Helpful hints

If the curtain tabs are hemmed, they can be sewn onto the outside of the curtain fabric with decorative buttons, to add an extra feature to the curtains.

11 Use a rule to check the length of the curtain drop—being careful to include the length of the tabs in your calculation—and then hand stitch the curtain hems along both sides and across the bottom of the curtain. Remove the pins that you used to secure the side hems in step 4.

12 Thread the curtain tab loops onto the curtain rod. Your curtain is now ready for hanging.

Helpful hints

If you need to block out strong sunlight, use black lining fabric. Alternatively, brightly colored lining fabric makes the window look good from the outside.

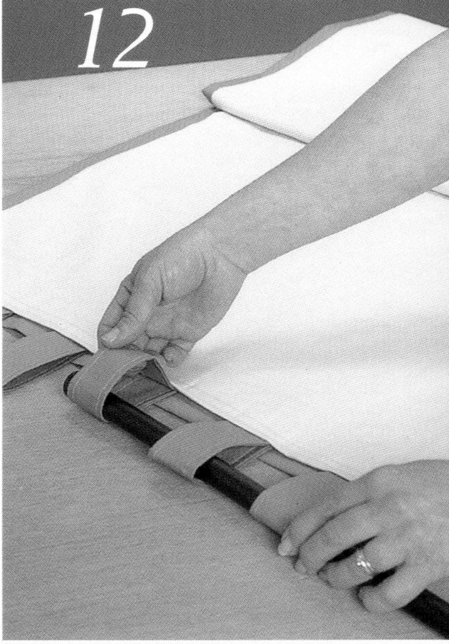

putting up a **wooden curtain pole**

One simple way to add a strong decorative feature to your living room is to enhance your windows and curtains by adding wooden curtain poles. These come in a variety of different woods, colors, and designs, and many of them have decorative finials on their ends. This project explains the easiest and most effective way to hang a wooden curtain pole.

Materials

Wooden curtain pole • Wooden brackets (usually supplied with the pole) • Wooden pole supports (usually supplied with the pole) • Wooden finials (usually supplied with the pole) • Wooden curtain rings (usually supplied with the pole) • Screws (usually supplied with the pole) • Wall plugs

Tools

Workbench • Tape measure • Plumb line • Spirit level • Combination square • Power drill with ¼ in. bit • Hand screwdriver • Hand saw • Hammer • Carpenter's pencil • Fine-grade abrasive paper and sanding block

Skill level

Beginner

Time

2 hours

1 Use a combination square and pencil to make a mark on the wall 3 in. up from the top edge of your window reveal and 2 in. to the outside of its upright edge. Repeat the process on the other side of the window. Run a measure or line between the two points and use a spirit level to check that they are level. Use a power drill with a ¼ in. bit to drill holes at both points to the depth of your wall plugs.

2 Use a hammer to tap the wall plugs gently into the holes that you drilled in step 1. The wall plugs will receive the screws that attach the brackets for the wooden curtain pole to the wall. Ensure that the wall plugs are tapped all the way in until their heads are flush with the surface of the wall.

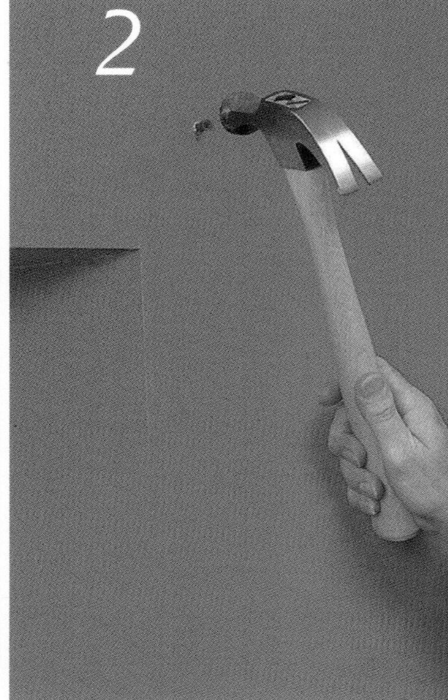

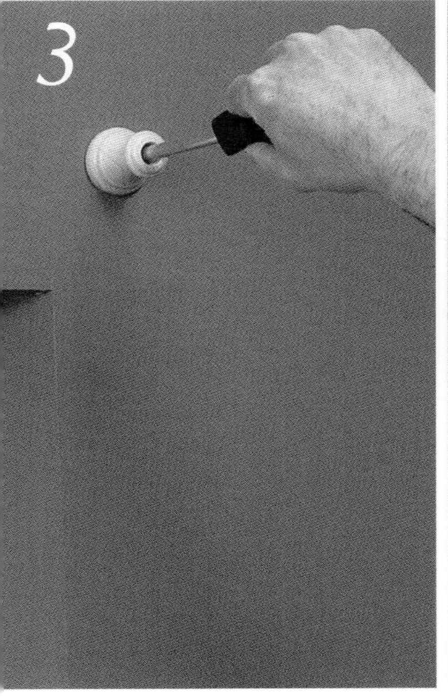

3 Use a hand screwdriver to attach the two wooden brackets to the wall, fixing the screws that are supplied with the curtain pole and brackets. Follow any particular manufacturer's instructions as you attach the brackets to the wall.

4 Most wooden curtain poles are supplied with pole supports, which receive the ends of the pole. Place these in position in the brackets on the wall, ensuring that their faces are square with each other. Secure the pole supports in place using the small screws that are supplied with the pole and its fittings.

5 Slide the wooden curtain pole into position between the pole supports and brackets, allowing 2 in. of pole to protrude from the outer edge of each of the pole supports. Mark off the length of the pole as necessary with a pencil. Remove the pole, clamp it into a workbench, and use a hand saw to cut off any excess length.

6 Once the pole has been cut to the correct length, sand off any rough edges at its ends and place it in position in the supports. Remove one end of the pole and hold it so that the pole remains horizontal. Slide all but two of the wooden curtain rings onto the pole, and return the end you are holding to the pole support.

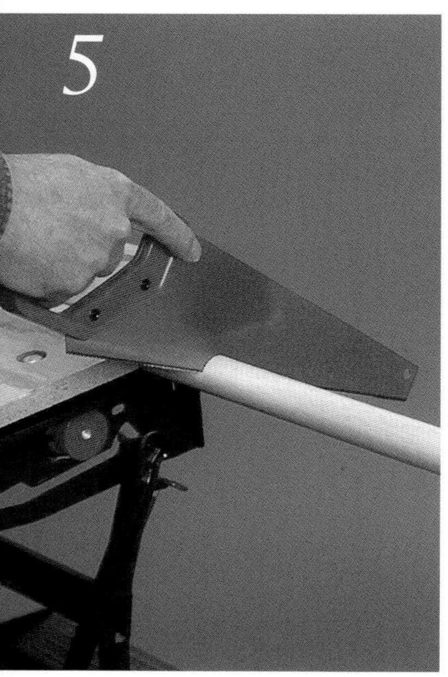
5

6

7 Slide the last two curtain rings onto the ends of the pole, where they protrude beyond the supports and brackets. These two end rings are held in place by the supports and finials, and prevent the outer curtain ends from being pulled right across the window. Take the two finials and slip them into place behind the last two curtain rings. Secure the pole in its correct position on the supports, using the small fixing screws that are supplied as part of the pole's fittings.

8 Finally, attach the curtain to the brass eyelets on the curtain rings, securing the end stops on the curtains to the last two rings between the pole supports and the finials.

making a cushion cover

Cushions are a quick and inexpensive way of adding a dash of color and style to your living room furniture. They are also an easy way of changing the look of your living room without too much effort. This cushion cover is easy to make and features a "no zipper" envelope closure.

Materials

Front of cushion: 1 piece of fabric 20 x 20 in.

Back of cushion: 2 pieces of fabric 20 x 14 in.

Cushion lining: 1 piece of fabric 20 x 20 in.;
2 pieces of fabric 20 x 14 in.

Cushion piping: 80 in. length of piping cord

Standard cushion pad to fit • Thread

Tools

Work surface • Electric sewing machine • Steam iron • Pins • Needle

Skill level

Intermediate

Time

4 hours

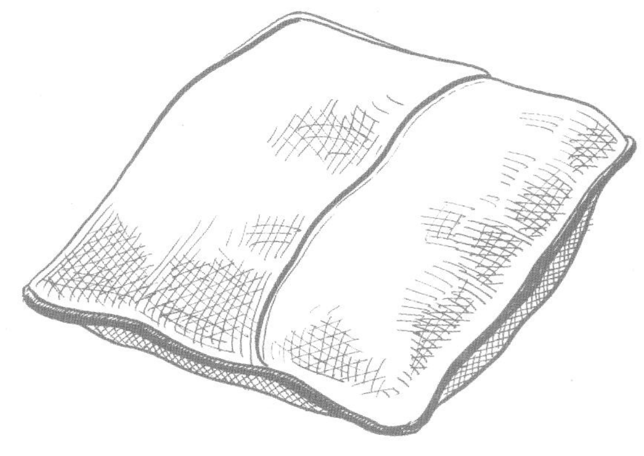

1 Cut all the pieces of fabric to the dimensions given in the list of materials. Take the front cushion cover piece and place it face down on the work surface. Cut a length of the piping cord equivalent to the combined lengths of the four sides of the square (80 in.). Pin the flat, material edge of the piping cord to the right-hand side of the square cushion cover piece, ensuring that it is fitted straight along the edge of the square, ½ in. in from its outside edge.

2 Loosely tack the piping cord in place by hand around the edge of the square, snipping around the excess flat fixing edge of the fabric where the corded, round piping joins the corners of the front cushion cover piece.

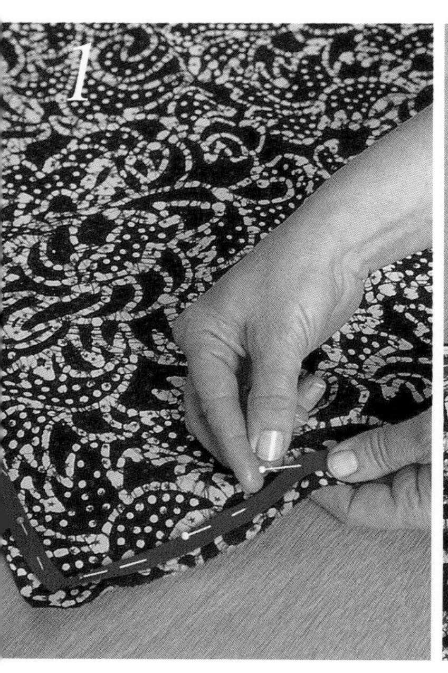
1

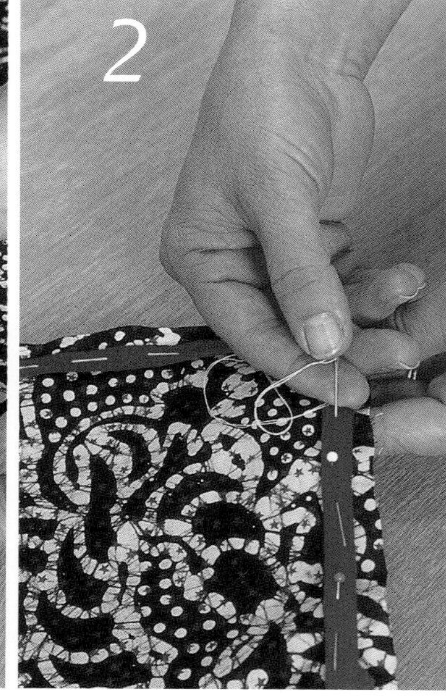
2

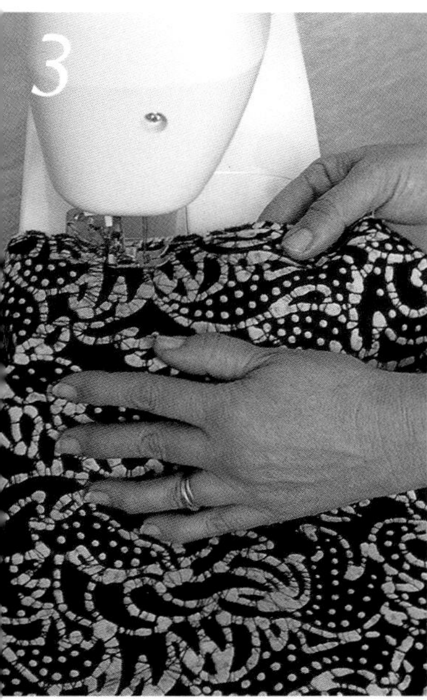

3 Take the two back pieces of the cushion cover and double-fold a ½ in. hem onto one 20 in. edge of each piece. Tack the hems and then use a zig-zag stitch on an electric sewing machine to secure them properly.

4 Place one back cushion cover piece with its stitched hem facing down onto the inside of the front piece. Pin it to the square, right up to the edge of the piping.

Helpful hints

Piping cord can be bought ready-covered in a range of plain colors, or made by enclosing narrow piping cord with any fabric of your choice.

5 Lay the other back cushion cover piece over the first one so that it is flush with the other end of the front piece, creating an overlap with the first back piece. Tack the two back pieces loosely together to secure them.

6 Use the sewing machine to stitch all round the edges of the cushion cover, joining the front piece to the back pieces, right up close to the piping. Ensure that you sew in a straight line and do not damage the piping.

Helpful hints

This method for making cushion covers is best-suited to lightweight materials, as in places along the side seams the needle must pass through four separate layers of fabric.

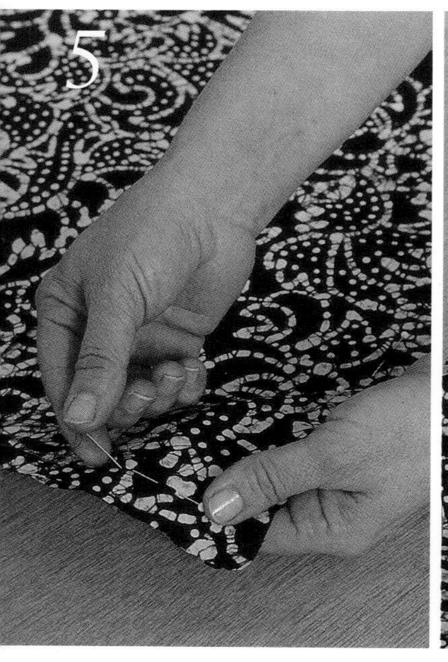

7 Once the pieces of the cushion cover have been sewn together, lay the cover on the work surface and use a hot steam iron to press the seams flat.

8 Insert the cushion pad into the aperture created by the fold that you made when you overlapped the back pieces in steps 4 and 5 and smooth the back pieces flat against each other. Your cushion is now ready for use.

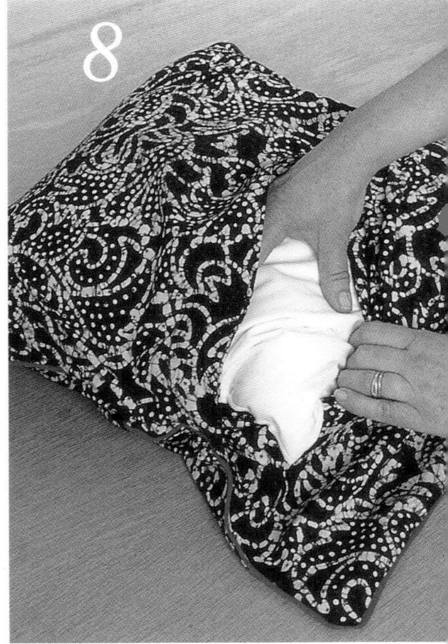

glossary

Batten—a narrow strip of wood, often used to describe such a strip used as a support for other pieces

Bevel—any angle other than a right angle at which two surfaces meet

Butt joint—a simple joint where two pieces of wood meet with no interlocking parts cut in them

Clearance hole—a hole drilled to the width of the screw shank, through which a screw passes before entering a pilot hole (*cf.*)

Countersink—to cut, usually drill, a hole that allows the head of a screw, nail, or pin to lie below the surface

Hardwood—wood cut from trees like oak, cherry, and elm, belonging to the botanical group *Angiospermae*

MDF—medium-density fiberboard; a prefabricated material that can be worked like wood

Miter—a joint made by cutting equal angles, usually at 45 degrees to form a right angle in two pieces of wood; cutting such a joint

PAR—"planed all round;" timber that has been planed smooth on all sides

Pilot hole—a small-diameter hole drilled into wood to act as a guide for a screw thread

Rebate—a stepped, usually rectangular, recess, cut along the edge of a piece of wood as part of a joint

Ripping—sawing wood along the grain

Softwood—wood cut from trees like pine, maple, and cedar, belonging to the botanical group *Gymnospermae*

Stencil—a transferable ink or paint pattern

Template—a cut-out pattern on paper or cardboard, used to help shape wood or transfer a pattern (*cf.* stencil)

Upright—a vertical piece of wood, usually part of a frame

index

acknowledgments

All photographs taken by Alistair Hughes, except for:

8/9 Elizabeth Whiting Associates; 38/39; 74/75 Camera Press Ltd.

Illustrations by Stewart Walton.